AN ENDURING FLAME

D0478887

AN ENDURING FLAME

The Brontë Story in Poetry and Photographs

Wendy Louise Bardsley

Photography by Simon Warner

First published in 1998 by
Smith Settle Ltd
Ilkley Road
Otley
West Yorkshire
LS21 3JP

Commentary and Selection of Poetry © Wendy Louise Bardsley 1998
Poems © The Poets 1998
Photographs © Simon Warner & Brontë Parsonage Museum 1998

ISBN   Paperback   1 85825 103 6
        Hardback   1 85825 104 4

British Library Cataloguing-in-Publication data:
A catalogue record for this book is available from the British Library.

Set in Gill Sans & Perpetua.

Designed, printed and bound by
SMITH SETTLE
Ilkley Road, Otley, West Yorkshire LS21 3JP

ACKNOWLEDGEMENTS

I am grateful to the Brontë Society and the Brontë Museum staff for their valuable assistance and allowing me the use of their Research Library. Also, I have found the books of scholarship by Elizabeth Gaskell, Winifred Gerin, Lyndall Gordon, Fanny Ratchford, Daphne du Maurier and Juliet Barker to be indispensable sources of information and enjoyment.

My thanks must go the the many authors and publishers who gave permission for the various poems to be reproduced. A full list of acknowledgements is on pages 151-156.

I would also like to thank Manchester Department of Libraries and Theatres, John Rylands University Library, Manchester, London Central Reference Library, the London Library, Bradford Local History Library, Tameside Central Reference Library, and the Manchester Metropolitan University Library for their considerable help. Finally, I must thank my friends and family for their interest and support, Christopher Reid and Ted Hughes for help and encouragement, Bloodaxe Books and *Envoi* magazine for constant vigilance and sending me poems, and Simon Warner for his marvellous photographs.

Wendy Louise Bardsley
Marple, Cheshire
May 1998

CONTENTS

FOREWORD: MAKING BRONTËS OF US ALL

I read *Wuthering Heights* for the first time when I was at college in the mid-seventies; at North Staffordshire Polytechnic to be precise, in a functional block of a building near the Weston Road Cemetery and not far from the Uttoxeter bus stop. It seemed a far cry (in a very literal sense) from Cathy and Heathcliffe and the windy hills, and I'm sure that my reading of *Wuthering Heights* was instrumental in my decision to go back to Yorkshire every weekend just to hear people who spoke like me.

Lots of people can point to the influence that the Brontës have had on them, but perhaps more importantly lots of creative people have used the Brontës as a springboard, as you can see and read in this book, and maybe that's the great thing about writing as good as the Brontës' writing: it doesn't exist in a vacuum, it inspires further work.

Of course, it's not just the writing that makes us excited about the Brontës, it's the lives lived on the moors, the creation of the private worlds, the almost impossibly romantic huddle of sisters and brother in the dark house; it would be difficult for such potent ingredients not to stir the imagination.

So this book, with its superb photographs and vast range of written responses, is a kind of map of how art can feed on art. How photographs and poems can be part of a continuum started in Haworth Parsonage and continued in notebooks and in cluttered studies and on the backs of buses (in my case) and in word processors. I think that it's how writing from the past should be used not just as a dead text on fading paper, but as a living example for us to use for our own creativity.

I've been working recently on a piece for improvised jazz bass and female voice, made up of found phrases from *Wuthering Heights*, and the odd thing is that I can dip into the book and fish out sentences that work really well in this context, and perhaps in any context … all I'm saying is that I think you should enjoy this book, but to enjoy it to the full you should use it as a touchpaper for your own creativity. Books can create poems can create photographs can create poems can create books, and the process started all those years ago in that imaginative hothouse in West Yorkshire will never end until imagination ends, which is never.

Ian McMillan

INTRODUCTION

The pathos and passion of the Brontë story excites love and admiration worldwide. Beginning with the noble journey of Patrick Brontë, moving from his poor Irish roots in County Down to study at Cambridge University, the story follows him through his various posts with the Church, ending finally with him outliving the whole of his family, having witnessed all their tragic deaths apart from Anne's.

But the Brontës live on through their writings. Literary endeavour seems to have been a constant occupation for all of them, Patrick often putting pen to paper when he could find the time, writing *Cottage Poems* and *The Cottage in the Wood* with marked simplicity for easy reading. Maria, his wife, and mother to the Brontë children, is also said to have attempted a long piece of writing, and her letters are skilfully and wittily created.

The story of Aunt (Elizabeth) Branwell's move in 1821, in her forties, from her comfortable home in Cornwall to the howling moors of Haworth, beautiful no doubt in summer, but quite treacherous in winter, to look after her dead sister's little children, is one of grace and virtue which she sustained until her death twenty years later.

The Parsonage Museum throbs with the energy of juvenilia created in a frenzy of collective creative inspiration, the children pouring out their vivid imaginations into art and literature. The lives of the Brontës alone is enough to arouse the deepest and most sincere of human emotions before we even begin to acknowledge the genius of their work. What strikes me most, however, about these quite unique people, is the perfect integrity between person and art.

Poetry stole a sizeable portion of the Brontë soul. Patrick, the parson and father to the children, published *The Cottage Poems* whilst working at St Peter's in Hartshead-cum-Clifton where Maria and Elizabeth, the first of the Brontë children, were born. He also wrote poetry inspired by natural and homely events, as for instance *The Phenomenon*, written in 1824 after an eruption on the bog at Crow Hill, and the sixty-six line *Tweed's Letter To His Mistress*, a verse 'letter' from a dog he was looking after for the Buckworths in Dewsbury.

The Brontë children were constantly creating stories, poems and plays in what Branwell called a 'scribblemania' — all this, Charlotte reflected on later, as having been like 'A web of sunny air'. The Brontë children were spared the labour of working in the factories as other children did, but often spent long and lonely hours together writing. Whilst sharing themes of love, loneliness and liberty, their individual interpretations were quite different. Emily's was often wild and untamed, Charlotte's more restrained, and Anne's religious and gentle. The sisters are mainly known for their prose writings, in particular the great masterpieces, *Jane Eyre* by Charlotte which tells the story of a young governess courageously refusing the coldly allotted place given to her by society, and Emily's *Wuthering Heights,* exploring the elemental and tragic plight of two young lovers who experience a relationship that takes them beyond the realms of the human world. Emily's mystical work in particular is peculiarly stirring in its vision and execution. The Brontë stories and poems are known throughout the world, as are the tragedies that walked beside them.

This book endeavours to bring together, for the first time, some of the poetry composed by poets throughout the world who have been inspired by the Brontës. The poems are taken from the nineteenth century up to modern times. Also included are poems written by the Brontës themselves, all poems placed where they fit naturally into the story. Images by the photographer Simon Warner capture the landscape known by the Brontës in all its moods and through the seasons. Together this selection of poems and photographs add a new and enjoyable dimension to the rich legacy of Brontë literature.

THE BRONTË HERITAGE

Today Haworth has become a memorial to the Brontë family, with a regular flow of visitors from around the world. Cafés and shops bear names of protagonists from the novels, and there is a vast literature consisting of biographies, plays, poetry, criticism and guides. Recently a ballet has laid claim to a place in the repertoire of Brontë inspiration, and also a musical. Who knows what else will come along in the future?

Towards the end of her life, Charlotte noted the enormous number of people coming to Haworth to see where the famous novels had been written, saying:

'... our rude hills and rugged neighbourhood will I doubt not form a sufficient barrier to the frequent repetition of such visits.'

The Parsonage, 1992

The steady warmth in these little rooms
    could never have been for them.
Though it may have seemed so, coming in
    from the rain's drench, the wind's attack.
They might have felt the same heat-
    recovering shiver down the back.

Close-matted boards receive our feet.
    For theirs, stone flags' ice chill
through turkey rugs, and through thin soles
    on dainty boots like these we so admire.
And think; these mittens lying next to them
    were meant for indoor wear.

True, there was the kitchen fire,
    good for drying shawls, toasting
chilblains to a blaze of agony.
    Good too for drawing close enough
within its arc of light and warmth
    their mingled genius. And breath ...

The rooms fill up. No chance now
    of a murmured word, scratch of pen,
a cough ... a rustle of skirt — perhaps
    of that incredibly tiny dress —
Whiff of whiskey? Baking bread? No.
    There is only what we see, like these

tiny words spelling confederacy
of childhood; a letter telling of an adult
    grief ... the immediacy of life's purpose
in a sketch of two of them working
    at table, this very one here before us ...
That couch in the corner, its darkness speaking

    of a well-documented ending ...
But where are they? A last look out
    at their daily view — grey graves absolved
by a veil of leaves — tells us, not there.
    And not here in this crowd, we somehow know.
Best go home and read. The books may show.

Patricia Adelman

Brontë Country

Even ordinary things
    lie enshrined
An old comb, pigments in a paint
    box, dry as stone
Emily's lamp, no larger
    than her hand, still seeks
the stair — small bedrooms where
    children pressed pale against the glass
look down
    to the churchyard
there, mother and sisters lie
    entombed

Wind still blows
    lapwing and moorland
grouse survive amid the gorse
    Over rainy heath rooks
fly. Ghosts, past peat-smoke from stone
    chimneys, sluice down the darkening sky
Settle, random chessmen
    on the graveyard's shouldering tablets
      Kenning, croaking
      shrouded as old women
      hunched over candles
      they pulse out again and again
in ancient argument with death
    a raucous distrust
      an abiding enmity
    against the slippage
      of day …

Marianne (Robertson) MacCuish

5

A Visit To Brontëland

The road climbs from the valley past the public
Park and turns, at the Haworth Co-operative Stores,
Into the grey stone village, and the steep
Street leading to the Parsonage, the inn, the WCs
To the Church of St Michael and All Angels,
   high in the trees.

The West Lane Baptists are putting on
Patience, the playbills say. The Heathcliff Tea-rooms are aglow
With English teachers in sensible tweeds. Bearded cyclists
Lean on their pedals, and their saddles shine and sway
Up the hill to the YHA.

Across the valley thick with mills
The fellside rises like an aerial map
Of fields and drystone walls and farms.
Pylons saunter over the minimum of fuss,
And round the bend from Keighley comes the Brontë bus.

An arty signboard poses Charlotte in a crinoline
And ringlets, penning Jane Eyre, at a table, with a quill,
'This must be "it"'. — The wandering Americans,
   like Technicolor ads,
Have reverence plainly written on their open faces.
They know just how one should behave in hallowed places.

A sea of scriptured slabs
Shines in the graveyard under the twilight rain.
The cold winds are crying in the trees.
New heights above the pines
Are wuthered by tractors of open-cast mines.

The church where the Brontës worshipped
Is long demolished. Only a brass plate
Marks where their bones are buried. Smothered
In Parks Committee geraniums, Anne lies along
In Scarborough Old Churchyard, under a dolled-up stone.

Now, in the village roofs, the television aerial aspires,
No idle toy would have tempted Branwell
From the 'Bull', and brandy; or kept that sister
From her tragic poems. They knew they had nothing but
   the moor
And themselves. It is we, who want all, who are poor.

James Kirkup

Dying Conditions at Haworth

Should have been healthy in high hill air;
no industrial pollution or
acid rain, good exercise
on steep hill streets; for some
walks under cloud-wild skies —
yet average lifespan equalled there
the unhealthiest parts of London.

Should have been healthy high on that hill
but water sources, scanty, poor quality
at best, grew poorer still in summer months
when lack of sewers, open cess-pits,
posed greater risk —
more than a third of local children
died before age of six.

Should have been healthy, home on high moor,
but flagstone floors draw damp in rain
and winter winds pierce wall, door, window;
father forbade warm carpets, curtains,
for fear of fire. He did not know
till later that disease, once in,
can burn through bodies, lungs,
as sure as flame.

Mary Hodgson

After Visiting the Brontë Parsonage

I dreamed last night of Haworth. Midnight.
Heard the church clock's knell to yesterday.

Saw from my bedroom window
rows of headstones, beckoning.

I chanted 'Our Father' over and over,
hoped its glazed façade would not shatter.

I remembered Abraham Sutcliffe
who 'hath two sittings in this pew'

no longer seated — prone and coffin framed,
his carpals pointing at me, a summons.

Alison Chisholm

Exhibits, Haworth Parsonage

Charlotte's wedding bonnet is empty now,
but a shy riot of grey lace flowers
still celebrates the end of long waiting,
the beginning of a life. A few
lilies-of-the-valley have almost escaped.

Her baby's bonnet is turned to the wall;
finely worked lace, white as lilies,
it is tiny, perfect, and empty.

Valerie Laws

The Brontës' Garden

Near the parsonage wall, they planted
the primitive, small-flowered Michaelmas daisy,
foxgloves and old-fashioned roses,
grown not for colour but scent.

It must look after itself, this garden;
few plants will thrive so high in Yorkshire,
and those that do, in such weather,
are necessarily tough.

Get off the coach, walk up that hill
and stay there, letting the crowds go past you.
Break a lavender head, savour
the dry dark smell of rosemary.

The records speak of elder and lilac,
a gravel path, not often weeded,
bushes where Emily or Anne,
each summer, picked blackcurrants.

They are all here, or their descendants,
and now you see, refurbished,
a garden of subdued colours —
dark green, pastel and silver.

Here also are the pines that Charlotte
planted on her wedding morning.
French-speaking visitors pass
beneath them, not looking.

She never saw the pines, but they
outlived her, and her baby.
Now someone else will plant a cone,
and the tree take root again.

Merryn Williams

At Haworth

Roots of cloudberry
among the nardus grass.
Gritstone for grinding
is lion shapes in the crags.
Walls shift and settle
as the moorland moves.

The gravestones sag,
battalions of them;
and the fortress line
of linked cottages
fronts horizontal wind,
diagonal rain.

No wonder the cobbles
huddle together
and flat slabs shield
those beds of dead.
Yet there are times when
the Parsonage glows
like topaz.

Gladys Mary Coles

TOWARDS HAWORTH

Before moving to Haworth, Patrick Brontë had been curate to the Reverend J Buckworth, vicar of All Saints, Dewsbury, in Yorkshire, having been placed there in 1809. Later, in 1811, he became vicar at St Peter's in Hartshead-cum-Clifton, where he met Maria Branwell who was to become his wife and the mother of the Brontë children. It was here that their first child, also named Maria, was born in 1814, and Elizabeth in 1815; and where Patrick published the first of his books, *The Cottage Poems*.

Patrick's aim in writing the book, was to provide reading that might reach the poorest and least able of readers, being printed in clear type with no more than sixteen lines to a page. He was happy at Hartshead, though it might have been more of an adjustment for Maria, having left the warm Cornish weather and her genteel lifestyle for the much harsher climate of Yorkshire and the hardier existence. Two years later, in 1815, Patrick exchanged livings with the Reverend Thomas Atkinson, the curate at Thornton near Bradford, where they moved to the small parsonage in Market Street. Here Charlotte (1816), Branwell (1817), Emily Jane (1818) and Anne (1820) were born. Maria Brontë had brought six children into the world in the space of just eight years.

Patrick then moved with Maria and the children, in 1820, to be curate at the church of St Michael and All Angels, Haworth, where the Reverend Grimshaw had preached fearless sermons a century before in the three-tiered pulpit.

The church has been rebuilt since the Brontës' day, and only the tower is part of the original structure. Also, when the family arrived there were no trees. In 1820, the parsonage, almost the last house in the village, looked out on a vast stretch of open moorland at the back. Today it is surrounded by modern houses and car parks, though the moors can still be seen from one of the windows.

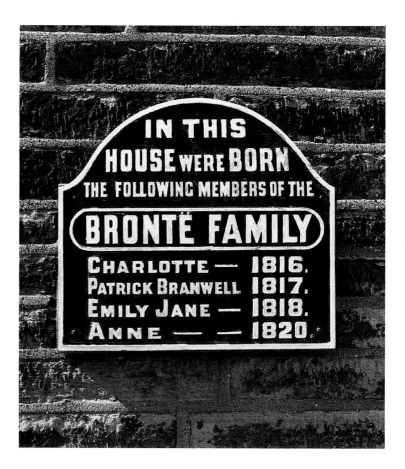

Mrs Brontë's Haworth Move

Picture the gig and seven heavy carts,
the planks' rattling clatter that eight-miled
April day. How high we'd piled the household
goods — pots, linen, crocks, clothes, Brontë's books —
our little six nursed between Nance and Sarah Garrs.

Emily, Bran and little Anne slept nearly all the way
till that last straining climb, horses chafing reins,
flanks fined to iron, hoofs clacking for hold on end-ways
paving slabs, the carrier's lads urging our lurching, wheels
screaling, and always that bump and thud of wood
until the almost-spill over the hill by the Black Bull.
As we turned, Maria keened at the house's stiff
symmetry, the central door, the slab-grey
stone oppressed beneath the weighty roofing flags.

Brontë (Lord be praised he'd concealed his brace
of pistols) was relieved to see sexton Brown waiting
with the keys — seems we're finally clear of Heap
and Redhead. Decorum's first — 'We've made good speed' —
the hall, must and dust confounding us, eyes panning
everyplace at once, unpapered walls, emptiness,
the yellow-stoned floor, the space. The chill.

Late evening saw an ordered ritual: lads carting
crates and box, Maria tottering under sermon-notes,
Brontë with his lofty rhymes, while Nance trimmed
the lamps and filled the hearths with flames, and Sarah
scratched a meal. Took hours after prayers to settle us.

Next morning, busied visiting 'the living' — the stern
church (how Brontë made the nave resound), gravestones
leaning almost to the house — we didn't notice Charlotte
slip away, but searching came upon her, plucked
daffodils bruising in her hand. Tip-toeing the garden wall
she scanned the watery moor-lines stretching before, beyond.
Reaching down, she asked, 'Is here our home for long?'
'God willing, yes. A fine house to grow you children in.'

Later, placing the flowers in the children's rooms,
I noticed the exhaustion-twinge searching my limbs.
Some rest, God grant it will not come again.

Roger Elkin

Tweed's Letter to his Mistress

Ah! Mistress dear,
Pray lend an ear,
To simple Robin Tweed;
I've been to you
Both kind and true,
In every time of need.
I have no claim,
To rank or name,
Among the barking gentry;
No spaniel neat,
Nor greyhound fleet,
To grace the street, or entry.
But then you know,
I still can shew,
A bonny spotted skin,
Can watch the house,
Kill rat or mouse,
And give you 'welcome in'.

Patrick Brontë

(The letter is sixty six lines of verse, coming to a
complimentary close with: 'Your kind and trusty
and humble dog, Robin Tweed, at my kennel near
the Vicarage, Dewsbury, the 11th June 1811.')

Whilst the children discovered great creative talents in themselves at this time, their lives were often to prove sad and pitiable. The first great blow was the death of their mother, Maria, in September 1821, from cancer, probably of the uterus. After Maria's death, Patrick became increasingly withdrawn and eccentric in his behaviour, taking his meals alone in his study and wearing a loaded pistol at all times of the day. He had a dread of fire and would have no curtains in the house. There are stories of him having sawn up chairs from his wife's bedroom when a confinement did not go right, and burning coloured shoes given to him for the girls because he thought they might make them vain.

Patrick Brontë was, however, to have a powerful role in the shaping of the minds of the children, and a reader of the biographical literature is hard-pressed to find any of his family criticising him. A poem he wrote during 1811 in Dewsbury, where he was looking after the Buckworth's dog whilst they were away, shows him in humorous and sensitive mood. But after his wife's death this side of his nature fell away, and he became increasingly solitary and morose.

HAWORTH

Born in Ireland on St Patrick's Day 1777, the eldest son of Hugh Brunty, a tenant-farmer, and Eleanor (or Alice as she was sometimes called), Patrick Brontë had shown himself to be a young man who could discipline his mind and dedicate himself to study. He became assistant schoolteacher at the age of sixteen at Drumbally-roney school in County Down, and later tutor to the sons of the Reverend Thomas Tighe, Vicar of Drumballyroney, who set him on the path to Cambridge University, where in 1801 he was admitted to St John's College. It was here, whilst studying for a Bachelor of Arts degree, that he decided to change his name to Brontë, some have suggested, after his hero, Nelson, who was made Duke of Brontë and King of Naples in 1799.

Opposite Haworth Parsonage was the church, its yard brimming with graves, and whilst the moors surrounded Haworth, the highly-productive woollen industry had resulted in the growth of factories and mills. Haworth was overpopulated, having as many as 7,000 people in the parish by 1853, 2,000 of which inhabited the small town. Haworth life depended on trade, and suffered during the Napoleonic wars and the industrial revolution. Plague, poor laws and infant mortality brought misery, Patrick himself being brought into close contact through the burying of his parishioners.

Haworth possessed a poor water supply, often non-existent in summer, the time when typhus epidemics broke out. There was only one privy to every four and a half houses, and instances of eight families using one privy were common. The parsonage had a double-seater privy in the yard, shared with the servants. Middens were also shared and the remains of slaughtered animals would be left to fester.

The Parsonage, Haworth

'In the earth, the earth though shalt be laid
A grey stone standing over thee;
  Black mould beneath thee spread
  And black mould to cover thee'
                    Emily Brontë

Gravestones piled deep as fallen leaves,
trodden into the sodden ground;
last consumptive flush of Autumn
in the sycamores;
a kissing-gate swings disused
in the bitter wind.

Cries of crows, rattle of rain,
on the nursery windowpane;
insistent tick of the grandfather clock,
insistent tock of the stonemason's hammer,
stammered epitaphs
swathed in lichened green.

It is not the stone that eats their bodies,
but the black spring that runs through them
that feeds the dark sarcophagus.

A glimpse of sun
sudden as a blush suffusing soft cheeks;
pale blue eyes
calling through blond coppices of hair
across the dimpled moors.

Adrian Henri

Haworth Parsonage, Mt Maunganui

(for E P D)

This house: *five headstones* — *five or any number*
of senses, of dead, of fingers of the left hand
or lost world not sharing the secret,
climb, strapped with sand, salt-fed, bloom
white, alive, upon a morning trellis of cloud,

make summer houses where the living
command the sun behind tall glass,
to warm, not set fire to their tombs autumn covering;
for leaves burn, mirrors break, Gerda-grime here
as in treeless Yorkshire may enflame their eyes.

Though never the five dead, coughing in fog
will feed this earth, yet, white stone your parsonage,
the house with its guavas, a lemon tree, hedge plants
wrapped in paper shawls against the frost; dank weed,
  castaway log,
sea-drowned wapiti antler the flower's full provision.

Janet Frame

24

Visit to Haworth

The moors were not so high
as I expected them to be,
the signs in Japanese
surprised me —
pointing the way

with the English ones —
to the Brontë Falls.
A cold journey ...
in shawls
the sisters had walked

further than they thought,
than they could imagine
even in childhood stories.
Found the sun
and garlands round them.

Shelah Florey

Haworth

The rooks wheeled and cawed
The tall elms like gaunt ghosts
The straight tomb-stones shadows
In the fog. I stumbled along the dark road
Went past the parsonage …

The road muddy; the sodden turf
Squeaking beneath my foot.
Suddenly clearing, the moors
Spread out. I began to breath
To run and run …

An old pale sun
Came peering through.

Ridley Beeton

No sewage system existed to carry off refuse, and decomposing matter and the exposed cesspools were very injurious to health. The *Babbage Report*, compiled after pressure from Patrick Brontë in 1850, gave the average age of death in the town as ranging from 20 to 31 years, and taken over twelve years, the average age of death was 26, corresponding with that of some of the most unhealthy of the London districts. Around forty-two per cent of the population born died before they were six years of age.

Haworth Moor

O wide, brown heath, bare hills, and lonesome dells,
 But ye are lovely in this amber light,
  Your shadows grim all mellowed in the bright
Warm sunshine, and the flush of your fair bells!

All round this moorland path the ground upswells,
 With some stray sheep amid the heather blooms;
  And with its dark, broad bulk, before us looms
The mighty Boulsworth. Where this streamlet wells

Through moss and fern, a sister band would roam,
 With fire of genius in
  their large bright eyes.
Peopling their free and boundless desert home
 With life which they alone beheld and heard,

Their sole companions the bee and bird,
 Within the round of these o'er-arching skies!

James Waddington

Brontë Bridge

So this is the place:
Stone slabs laid over a stream
And a trickle of water cutting a hillside —
Better when the snowmelts tumble no doubt
But pretty enough and cold on unbooted feet.

To this place the children came,
Charlotte, Emily, Branwell and Anne,
Living their wild life in imagination,
Thrown in on each other's company,
Thought a bit queer by local folk.

To this place also Charlotte walked,
Pregnant and alone when the rest were dead.
She did not long survive that last visit.
Now signs mark the route she took
And Sunday strollers make their pilgrimage.

They find it further than expected,
Wish for flatter shoes, struggle with buggies.
Children splash and squeal in the water
While a girl sits, plugged to synthetic sound.
She does not hear the water's soft conversation,

Yet in our different ways we each pay homage,
If only with unaccustomed effort,
Leaving cars and ice-cream vans behind.
Charlotte, Emily, Branwell and Anne,
We remember you.

Pauline Kirk

Brontë Way

Was it like this then —
bog-cotton milk maids
purple and silver grass
a curlew's continual song
punctuated by sheep cries?
Did she stride uncaring
through boggy patches
in unsuitable shoes
lie face up to the sun
as I do now eyes closed
friends' voices a murmur
behind a stone wall?
Did she seek her Spirit
giver of great poems
and one strange novel
on such high June days
brief in intense beauty
between the darkness.

Jean Barker

Haworth and the parsonage were to have a profound effect on the Brontë children. From a school near Dewsbury, Charlotte writes:

> 'I am just going to write because I cannot help it. Wiggins [a name she called Branwell] might indeed talk of scribblemania if he were to see me just now … that wind, pouring impetuous current through the air, sounding wildly, unremittingly from hour to hour, deepening its tone as the night advances, coming not in gusts, but with a rapid gathering stormy swell — that wind I know is heard at this moment far away on the moors of Haworth. Branwell and Emily hear it, and as it sweeps over our house, down the churchyard, and round the old church, they think perhaps of me and Anne.'

Patrick constantly worried about his health. The parsonage would provide the children with a home whilst he lived, but if he died, they would be rendered homeless since the house belonged to the church. He thought several times about marrying again and made a couple of proposals which were turned down. Eventually, Maria's older sister Elizabeth Branwell made what seems now to have been an immense sacrifice and life-long commitment to her sister's motherless children. She came all the way from Penzance, as her sister had done before her, to Yorkshire, where she took up residence with the Brontë family in 1821, staying until her death in 1842.

AUNT BRANWELL

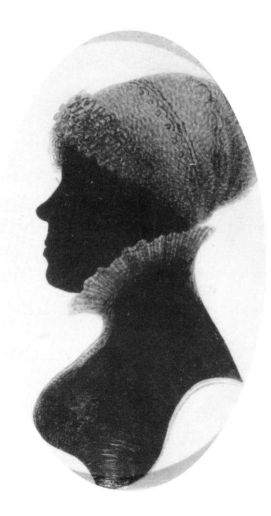

Aunt (Elizabeth) Branwell had a private income of her own. She was a well-educated woman, and soon became a mother figure to the Brontë children with an important role in the shaping of their minds and behaviour. As her sister before her, she too must have felt the contrast between the stark and often damp Yorkshire moorland and her sunny home in Penzance. At the parsonage she had her own bed-sitting room where she often shut herself away. Having been summoned to the house by Patrick when her sister was seriously ill, she no doubt felt bewildered by the profound tragedy that had befallen the family. The small children were fearful of making any sound whilst their mother was lying ill in the bedroom, and must have wondered what was happening. 'My poor children, my poor children', she had whispered on her dying breath at just thirty eight years of age, the age at which Charlotte, outliving all her siblings, was also to die.

At this time the children were taken ill with scarlet fever, Patrick writing that 'something sickened my whole frame … of such a nature as cannot be described …'

The sense of duty that had brought Elizabeth Branwell to Haworth was in keeping with many of Patrick's own moral leanings, and the two of them held many common beliefs. With Aunt Branwell and their father often shut away in their rooms and the servants in theirs, the children were frequently thrown on their own resources, thereby allowing for the development of the creativity that flooded from the combination of their highly intelligent and sensitive minds.

Aunt Branwell used her bedroom as a classroom where she taught the girls how to sew samplers and repair clothes. They also drew, practised music and discussed current affairs through the reading of *Blackwood's*, the

High Waving Heather

High waving heather, 'neath stormy blasts bending,
Midnight and moonlight and bright shining stars;
Darkness and glory rejoicingly blending,
Earth rising to heaven and heaven descending,
Man's spirit away from its drear dungeon sending,
Bursting the fetters and breaking the bars.

All down the mountain-sides, wild forests lending
One mighty voice to the life-giving wind;
Rivers their banks in the jubilee rending,
Fast through the valleys a reckless course wending,
Wilder and deeper their waters extending,
Leaving a desolate desert behind.

Shining and lowering and swelling and dying,
Changing for ever from midnight to noon;
Roaring like thunder, like soft music sighing,
Shadows on shadows advancing and flying,
Lightning-bright flashes the deep gloom defying,
Coming as swiftly and fading as soon.

Emily Brontë

Emily Jane Bronte May the 2ᵈ 1829

Lady's Magazine and other pamphlets, forming opinions on political, domestic and artistic issues. Aunt Branwell became an integral and indispensable part of her sister's family, she and Patrick giving lessons to the children until it was felt they needed a more formal education.

The older girls were sent to a school at Crofton near Wakefield for a time, but were later withdrawn, going then to a new clergy daughter's school at Cowan Bridge some fifty miles away. The school provided full board and tuition to daughters of poor clergymen, and was a semi-charitable institution making it possible for Patrick to pay. Here they might learn how to become governesses, which was likely to be the only occupation available to them. The four sisters, Maria, ten and a half, Elizabeth, nine, Charlotte, eight, and Emily, six and a half, were amongst the first pupils at Cowan Bridge School. Anne was still a baby at this time, and Branwell continued his studies with his father acting as tutor.

The Reverend Carus Wilson, the school's founder and a wealthy landowner, had a large house named Casterton Hall near the school. He was well known in educational and evangelical circles, although the ideas he held were in opposition to those of Patrick Brontë. Wilson believed, as many did at the time, that children had sinful natures and should be constantly corrected. The supply of food was meagre and the rooms cold. The children were also forced to take walks in the outdoors, often in poor weather. It was not long before the Brontë children were taken ill, Maria first, developing tuberculosis and having to return home, where she died.

Gondal

Listen! I can hear children laughing
their voices silver tinsel amid the corded plush.
In the whitewashed study-playroom
time has turned itself inside out,
lifting the latch of a painted door
hung with shawls and collected heather sprays.
Tongues askew, they are scribbling again
across and across those microscopic notebooks,
straining the bossy girl's weak sight,
the other two's heads together, but
it's undoubtedly the boy who dominates.
His eyes are coals in a pallid face
febrile with excitement. Red haired,
red handed, he slays his Young Men
on the playing fields of Waterloo.
But the girls have created Gondal,
the secret world to which they may invite him
since he's good with ghosts and gibbets,
assaulting them with his erudition
if he doesn't frighten himself first
into one of his vomiting fits.

Now they are all writing, writing …
Listen! I can hear children creating …

Lewis Hosegood

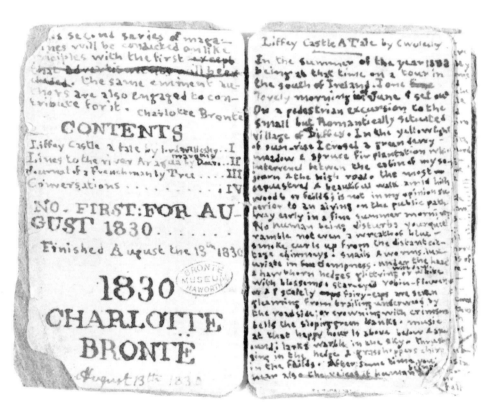

Retrospection

We wove a web in childhood,
    A web of sunny air;
We dug a spring in infancy
    Of water pure and fair;

We sowed in youth a mustard seed,
    We cut an almond rod;
We are now grown up to riper age:
    Are they withered in the sod?

Are they blighted, failed and faded,
    Are they mouldered back to clay?
For life is darkly shaded,
    And its joys fleet fast away.

Faded! the web is still of air,
    But how its folds are spread,
And from its tints of crimson clear
    How deep a glow is shed.
The light of an Italian sky
Where clouds of sunset lingering lie
    Is not more ruby-red.

But the spring was under a mossy stone,
    Its jet may gush no more.
Hark! sceptic bid thy doubts be gone,
    Is that a feeble roar
Rushing around thee? Lo! the tide
Of waves where armed fleets may ride
Sinking and swelling, frowns and smiles
An ocean with a thousand isles
    And scarce a glimpse of shore.

The mustard-seed in distant land
    Bends down a mighty tree,
The dry unbudding almond-wand
    Has touched eternity.
There came a second miracle
Such as on Aaron's sceptre fell,
And sapless grew like life from heath,
Bud, bloom and fruit in mingling wreath
All twined the shrivelled off-shoot round
As flowers lie on the long grave-mound.

Dream that stole o'er us in the time
When life was in its vernal clime,
Dream that still faster o'er us steals
    As the mild star of spring declining
The advent of that day reveals.
    That glows on Sirius' fiery shining:
Oh! as thou swellest, and as the scenes
    Cover this cold world's darkest features,
Stronger each change my spirit weans
    To bow before thy god-like creatures.

Charlotte Brontë

In later years, Charlotte often reflected on the precious days of her childhood at the parsonage. She wrote this poem in 1835 while a teacher at Miss Wooler's school, Roe Head, when she was nineteen years of age.

Cowan Bridge Boarding School

It would have reassured the parson
that Hannah More and Wilberforce
were patrons of the school
where his motherless daughters went —
Maria (his avid newspaper reader)
and Elizabeth,
who might have governed life

at the parsonage,
rescued Branwell from himself.
Now footnotes to their siblings' fame
their deaths at eleven and ten
in the same year, forty days apart,
shadows no sun can penetrate,
dipped pens in tears and pain.

Peggy Poole

At Cowan Bridge

(for Elsa Corbluth)

This place has elected to lie low.
Houses are called Private Road
and Private Property.

Everything is ostentatiously eating:
Free-ranging hens and geese, a fat horse,
A goat tethered to its larder.
Black-snouted lambs nuzzle and crop.
The local store sells local lemon curd.
Two miles away at the teashop they hope
To delight your palate, and restore
Those jaded tastebuds.

And dandelions do well. Their mop heads stare
Up at the sun. But the scrawny ash
Hugs back its green.

Discreet of you not to die here,
Maria, Elizabeth, elder daughters,
Who caught death here.
The river's a true witness. It sings
A bleak song: children were cold here,
And children were hungry. The lion-headed fell

Averts its gaze, but you can see where winter
Has rubbed it raw. Here children died.

But were buried elsewhere. Here discretion
Is expected of the dead. Outside the chapel
Jesus assures the longing lorries, in a dying fall.
I am the resurrection and the life
At Easter, in late hot April.
It makes no difference. Not many birds are singing.

What resurrection for the chilled children,
Blighted and broken, bundled home to die.
Killed off between July and June,
Silent singers, aged ten, aged nine?

Flesh is finished with. Something persists
In a sister, unrelenting, stunted;
In a dead child's voice outside a midnight window
Crying Let me in, let me in.

Here daffodils come
And have lived to regret it. In dwarfish clumps
They glower along the verge.

U A Fanthorpe

Thorp Green

I sit, this evening, far away
From all I used to know,
And nought reminds my soul to-day
Of happy long ago.

Unwelcome cares, unthought-of fears,
Around my room arise;
I seek for suns of former years,
But clouds o'ercast my skies.

Yes — Memory, wherefore does thy voice
Bring old times back to view,
As thou wouldst bid me not rejoice
In thoughts and prospects new?

I'll thank thee, Memory, in the hour
When troubled thoughts are mine —
For thou, like suns in April's shower,
On shadowy scenes wilt shine.

I'll thank thee when approaching death
Would quench life's feeble ember,
For thou wouldst even renew by breath
With thy sweet word 'Remember!'

Branwell Brontë

Alone I Sat

Alone I sat; the summer day
Had died in smiling light away;
I saw it die, I watched it fade
From misty hill and breezeless glade;

And thoughts in my soul were gushing,
And my heart bowed beneath their power;
And tears within my eyes were rushing
Because I could not speak the feeling,
The solemn joy around me stealing
in that divine, untroubled hour.

I asked myself: 'O why has heaven
Denied the precious gift to me,
The glorious gift to many given
To speak their thoughts in poetry?'

'Dreams have encircled me', I said,
'From careless childhood's sunny time;
Visions by ardent fancy fed
Since life was in its morning prime'.

But now, when I had hoped to sing,
My fingers strike a tuneless string;
And still the burden of the strain
Is: 'Strive no more: 'tis all in vain'.

Emily Brontë

Maria Brontë's death was soon followed by that of her sister Elizabeth. Maria was just eleven years old and Elizabeth ten.

The death of his daughters caused Patrick to fall into an even deeper depression, and the remaining children suffered greatly from the loss of their sisters. Branwell in particular was profoundly affected by the death of Maria, writing:

> 'What was that star which seemed to rise
> To light me on and guide me through?
> What was that form so heavenly fair,
> Untouched by time, unmarked by love.
> To whose fond heart I clung to save
> My sinking spirit from its grave'.

At this time the Brontë family began to close in on itself. Only Aunt Branwell and their father taught the children. It was now that they began to weave their 'web of childhood', as their imaginations grew and were inspired and their extraordinary ability as writers began to develop.

HAPPENINGS

On the evening of Thursday the 2nd September 1824, whilst Branwell, Emily and Anne had been out walking on the moors, a thunderstorm occurred and the bog at Crow Hill erupted, sending floods of muddy water and boulders down the hillside. Patrick saw this as divine intervention, telling his parishioners:

> 'We have just seen something of the mighty power of God; he has unsheathed his sword, and brandished it, over our heads, but still the blow is suspended in mercy — it has not yet fallen upon us …'

There had been overwhelming heat, thunder and lightning, and heavy rain at the time of the eruption, and the moor had been very wet for a number of years where it happened. Beneath the land there were reserves of water which may have expanded with the heat, thereby causing the tremor and outpouring of water. Patrick explores the event with a pamphlet he calls *The Phenomenon, or Account in Verse of the Extraordinary Disruption of a Bog*. The pamphlet was to be a Sunday school prize book.

from *The Phenomenon*

Now cawing rooks on rapid pinions move,
For their lov'd home, the safe sequester'd grove;
Far inland scream the frighten'd sea-gulls loud,
High the blue heron sails along the cloud;
The humming bees, sagacious, homewards fly,
The conscious heifer snuffs the tempest nigh:
But see! the hazy sun has reached the west,
The murmuring trees proclaim the coming blast.
Fast dusty whirlwinds drive along the plain,
The gusty tempest gives the slacken'd rein;
Low bend the trees, the lofty steeples rock,
And firmest fabrics own the sullen shock.
Condensing fast, the black'ning clouds o'erspread
the low'ring sky; the frequent lightning red,
With quivering glance, the streaming clouds do sunder,
And rumbles deep, and long, and loud, the thunder!
The tempest gathering from the murky west,
Rests on the peak, and forms a horrid crest.
Down pour the heavy clouds their copious streams,
Quick shoots the lightning's fiercely vivid gleams;
And loud and louder peals the crashing thunder;
The mountains shake as they would rend asunder,

But, see! the solid ground, like ocean driven,
With mighty force by the four winds of heaven,
In strange commotion rolls its earthy tide —
Whilst the river mountain from its rugged side,
A muddy torrent issues, dark and deep,
That foaming, thunders down the trembling steep!
As high on Alpine hills, for ages past,
The falling snows, pil'd by the stiff'ning blast,
Rise a huge mountain on the dazzl'd eye,
Just oe'r their base, far curling in the sky;
Till, by their weight, these mighty masses fall,
And breaking, thunder down the trembling vale;
Bury whole towns in everlasting snow,
And chill with horror pale, the world below,
So rocks on rocks, pil'd by the foaming flood,
All its vast force with trembling base withstood;
Till the indignant waves collecting fast,
Form'd a dark lake, urged by the incumbent blast;
And push'd at once, with wide resistless sway,
The mighty mass, 'midst thund'ring sounds, away;
Shook all the neighbouring hills, and thrill'd with fear,
The peasant's heart, and stunn'd his listening ear!

Patrick Brontë

43

Branwell Brontë is Re-incarnated as a Vest

I hang here like a ghost
on the midnight line;

frost hardens me, hardens the frocks
I hang with.

Irony to hang here on
a night crashing with the loud moon,

the moon only I can hear.

I hang here like a ghost
on the midnight line;

If you stand by the garden shed,
there, that side of the garden shed

and look at me from that angle,
look towards the washing line from that angle,

I'm almost invisible behind the frocks.

I hang here like a ghost.
The frost hardens
and dawn is dark years away.

Ian McMillan

Charlotte Brontë

The wind was blowing over the moors,
And the sun shone bright upon heather and whin,
On the grave-stones hoary and gray with age
Which stand about Haworth vicarage,
And it streamed through a window in.

There, by herself, in a lonely room —
A lonely room which once held three —
Sat a woman at work with a busy pen,
'Twas the woman all England praised just then
But what for its praise cared she?

Fame cannot dazzle or flattery charm
One who goes lonely day by day.
On the lonely moors, where the plovers cry,
And the sobbing wind as it hurries by
Has no comforting word to say.

So, famous and lonely and sad she sat,
And steadily wrote the morning through;
Then, at stroke of twelve, laid her task aside
And out to the kitchen swiftly hied.
Now what was she going to do?

Why, Tabby, the servant, was 'past her work',
And her eyes had failed as her strength ran low,
And the toils, once easy, had one by one
Become too hard, or were left half-done
By the aged hands and slow.

So every day, without saying a word,
Her famous mistress laid down the pen,
Re-kneaded the bread, or silently stole
The potatoes away in their wooden bowl,
And pared them all over again.

She did not say, as she might have done,
'The less to the larger must give way,
These things are little, while I am great;
And the world will not always stand and wait
For the words that I have to say.'

No; the clever fingers that wrought so well,
And the eyes that could pierce to the heart's intent,
She lent to the humble task and small;
Nor counted the time as lost at all,
So Tabby were but content!

Ah, genius burns like a blazing star,
And Fame has an honeyed urn to fill;
But the good deed done for love, not fame,
Like the water-cup in the Master's name,
Is something more precious still.

Susan Coolidge (Sarah Chauncey Woolsey)

Emily Brontë

The wind on Crow Hill was her darling.
His fierce, high tale in her ear was her secret,
But his kiss was fatal.

Through her dark Paradise ran
The stream she loved too well
That bit her breast.

The shaggy sodden king of that kingdom
Followed through the wall
And lay on her love-sick bed.

The curlew trod in her womb.

The stone weighed under her heart.

Her death is a baby-cry on the moor.

Ted Hughes

from *On Halley's Comet*

Our blazing guest, long have you been,
To us, and many more, unseen;
Full seventy years have pass'd away
Since last we saw you, fresh and gay —
Time seems to do you little wrong —
As yet, you sweep the sky along,
A thousand times more glib and fast,
Than railroad speed or sweeping blast —
Not so — the things you left behind —
Not so — the race of human kind,
Vast changes in this world have been,
Since by this world you last were seen:
The child who clapped his hands with joy,
And hailed thee as a shining toy,
Has pass'd long since, that dusky bourn,
From whence no travellers return;
Or sinking now in feeble age,
Surveys thee, as a hoary sage;
Sees thee, a mighty globe serene,
Wide hurried o'er the welkin sheen …

Patrick Brontë

Haworth Moor

('My sister Emily loved the moors')

The dark clouds pile above the misty moors
Into strange shapes and the keen wind blows cold.
Through it is summer; like mysterious doors
The hills in secret distances unfold.

This is a haunted land and a stern country;
The landscapes here seem vast and menacing
Under the sharp airs and the wheeling sky,
And man becomes remote, an alien thing.

Far from the crowded herd-life of the towns,
Their vain loud tumult and their garish joy;
The veiled horizons lift their giant crowns,
Whose peace and most sacred Time cannot destroy.

Out of this distance leapt that book of flame,
When to thy pure white forehead, Emily,
The dread winged Genius of these lorn hills came,
Kissed thee and sealed thee for Eternity.

Then from the marriage of thy mind with this
Land desolate and primaeval, from the morn
Streaming with tattered clouds, in rage and bliss,
The high exalted awful tale was born.

Within whose covers there is agony,
Fierce souls that seem to tear themselves and fail
Forever, and an ancient purity,
And pity poured like rain upon it all

From thy compassionate heart and daring thought.
The green earth with her all-embracing breast.
Tempest and dews and snow, and all things brought
At last beyond Death into endless rest.

The thunder and the wrath, the deeps of fire,
The roaring of the wind so beyond the world,
The essence and the spirit of sweet Desire,
The very beating heart of Love uncurled,

The crying of the eagle to his mate,
The moaning of the doves in sunlit trees,
The becks that glitter in their Autumn spate,
The wine-red heath-bells haunted by the bees.

Wilfred Childe

Up on the Moors with Keeper

Three girls under the sun's rare brilliance
out on the moors, hitching their skirts
over bog-myrtle and bilberry.

They've kicked up their heels at a dull brother
whose keep still can't you? *wants to fix*
them to canvas. Emily's dog stares at these

three girls under the juggling larks
pausing to catch that song on a hesitant wind,
all wings and faces dipped in light.

What could there be to match this glory?
High summer, a scent of absent rain,
away from the dark house, father and duty.

Maura Dooley

On Haworth Moor

Top Withens. These are the wuthering heights:
moors that on this perfect walking day
are hospitable in being empty
far as the horizon, the cloud they merge in.
Up here we might imagine like anyone
three dutiful daughters set loose to be
themselves and more than that in the opening out
of lives peopled by characters, tiny seeds
of a disease that flourished, biding its short time.
Their mother dead before she knew them,
Their father had God to answer to, and unanswered.
And so here they are, their dog, Keeper,
an excuse to be with us walking
a wayward, invented, grey-green path
guided by fiction, bits of biography.
The youngest of the three is missing,
disappointed, unremarked, thirty years old,
she lies on a blue velveteen sofa
in a cold room, admitting the doctor only in terror
hours before she died. The middle girl also
vanished. No search will discover her,
however exhaustive, however inspired;
nor the eldest, who outlived them ten years
to marry and to wander here, bundled in
words that broke her heart, recalling them
and the brother they made not famous.
Our little warmth of reconstruction,
the thousands that pay this same homage,
cannot hope to keep out the slight chill
that killed her and the child she carried,
however faithfully we remember
what we think we know, or say out loud
under a lightening sky her living name.

Peter Sansom

UNFOLDING DESTINIES

The rural society was over by the time Branwell was a young man. His education had been entirely academic, and he was ill-fitted for what was a rapidly changing society. The only boy of the family — having considerable talents, and on whom all hopes rested — Branwell often worked with his father translating. He must, however, have felt a great weight of responsibility at this time, and being a sensitive, gregarious person, would have been quite lonely, cut off for long periods from his family and other people.

There is a legend that, discovering he had a talent for painting, Branwell was encouraged to travel to London in order to present himself at the Royal Academy, the family having gathered together the money to send him.

P B Bronte

July 21 1833

To Imagination

So hopeless is the world without
The world within I doubly prize —
Thy world where guile and hate and doubt
And cold suspicion never rise —
Where thou and I and Liberty
Hold undisputed sovereignty.

Emily Brontë

I Am the Only Being

I am the only being whose doom
No tongue would ask, no eye would mourn;
I never caused a thought of gloom,
A smile of joy, since I was born ...

First melted off the hope of youth
Then fancy's rainbow fast withdrew,
And then experience told me truth
In mortal bosoms never grew.

'Twas grief enough to think mankind
All hollow, servile, insincere —
But worse to trust to my own mind
And find the same corruption there.

Emily Brontë

Portrait

Three sisters glare, Yorkshire defiance
extinguished hereditary trace
of Irish fancy.
Faces are blank slabs
just short of sneers, curls custom-coiled,
eyes disdaining all but middle-distance.

Animation was the brother
painted centre, his vivacity
delicious sin of gambling,
gin, seduction, debt. Perhaps
restraint of brushwork forced
frustrated blotting-out.

Still his presence ghosts the canvas,
dares a dissipated death,
denies creep of consumption.
He oversees, vital; refuses
to let oil choke; lives,
snatches the last laugh.

Alison Chisholm

According to the story, Branwell's journey to London was something of a disaster, and he returned home penniless with a variety of dubious and bizarre explanations. The tale is nowadays thought to be apocryphal.

Branwell was, however, poor. He was an intellectual, and unless he achieved greatness, he would always be poor. His letters to the editors of *Blackwoods Magazine*, where he offered his services as a writer, were almost always unanswered. Many were frantic and desperate:

'Now, Sir, to you I appear writing with conceited assurance: but I am not for I know myself so far as to believe in my own originality …'

The great Wordsworth also received a letter from him:

'… I most earnestly entreat you …'

Again there was a stony silence, Wordsworth apparently finding the letter sycophantic and ungracious in that Branwell claimed many poets of the day weren't worth sixpence.

Branwell's main talent seemed to lie in painting, and he decided to try to make it his living. The family paid for him to have lessons in Leeds with William Robinson, an outstanding Yorkshire artist who believed in Branwell and with whom Branwell had made a serious attempt at portrait painting. The well-known painting of his sisters, where a fourth person — almost certainly Branwell himself — appears brushed out, was done at this time, and may be indicative of Branwell's sense of failure.

Two Views of Withens

Above whorled, spindling gorse,
Sheepfoot-flattened grasses,
Stone wall and ridgepole rise
Prow-like through blurs
Of fog in that hinterland few
Hikers get to:

Home of the uncatchable
Sage hen and spry rabbit,
where second wind, hip boot
Help over hill
And hill, and through peaty water,
I found bare moor,

A colourless weather,
And the house of Eros
Low-lintelled, no palace;
You, luckier,
Report white pillars, a blue sky,
The ghosts, kindly.

Sylvia Plath

Ponden Kirk

Emily Brontë's Penistone Crag

Ponden Kirk — the Druid stones
Neither tower nor spire, owns, —
Rugged rocks of Nature's forming
Stands up naked to her storming
Sheer its depth to gorge below —
High above it wild winds blow
Sky and moors meet all around —
Here was Emily often found!

Book in hand and dog at heel! —
Solitude — her love, her zeal,
Here, she gave her great Creation
Drama, character, sensation!
High above the world, remote,
Sitting on this crag, she wrote,
'Mid the atmospheric powers
Beauty of the wild heath flowers!

None but a great Soul could achieve!
Wilderness, wild make believe,
Drawn in terrifying fashion
Give them stirring inner passion,
Depth of life's experience gained
To inspiring heights attained: —
HEATHCLIFF, brooding-sullen-dark-
Love to last beyond Time's mark!

Gladys Doreena Wilkinson

Hardcastle Crags

Flintlike, her feet struck
Such a racket of echoes from the steely street,
Tacking in moon-blued crooks from the black
stone-built town, that she heard the quick air ignite
its tinder and shake

A firework of echoes from wall
To wall of the dark, dwarfed cottages.
But the echoes died at the back as the walls
Gave way to fields and the incessant seethe of grasses
Riding in the full

Of the moon, manes to the wind,
Tireless, tied, as a moon-bound sea
Moves on its root. Through a mist-wraith wound
Up from the fissured valley and hung shoulder-high
Ahead, it fattened

To no family-featured ghost,
Nor did any word body with a name
The blank mood she walked in. Once past
The dream-people village, her eyes entertained no dream,
And the sandman's dust

Lost lustre under her footsoles.
The long wind, paring her person down
To a pinch of flame, blew its burdened whistle
In the whorl of her ear, and like a scooped-out pumpkin crown
Her head cupped the babble.

All the night gave her, in return
For the paltry gift of her bulk and the beat
Of her heart, was the humped indifferent iron
Of its hills, and its pastures bordered by black stone set
On black stone. Barns

Guarded broods and litters
Behind shut doors; the dairy herds
Knelt in the meadow mute as boulders;
Sheep drowsed stoneward in their tussocks of wool, and birds,
Twig-sleeping, wore

Granite ruffs, their shadows
The guise of leaves. The whole landscape
Loomed absolute as the antique world was
Once, in its earliest sway of lymph and sap,
Unaltered by eyes,

Enough to snuff the quick
Of her small heat out, but before the weight
Of stones and hills of stones could break
her down to mere quartz grit in that stony light
She turned back.

Sylvia Plath

Wuthering Heights

Walter was guide. His mother's cousin
Inherited some Bronte soup dishes.
He felt sorry for them. Writers
Were pathetic people. Hiding from it
And making it up. But your transatlantic elation
Elated him. He effervesced
Like his rhubarb wine kept a bit too long:
A vintage of legends and gossip
About those poor lasses. Then,
After the Rectory, after the chaise longue
Where Emily died, and the midget hand-made books,
The elvish lacework, the dwarfish fairy-work shoes,
It was the track from Stanbury. That climb
A mile beyond expectation, into
Emily's private Eden. The moor
Lifted and opened its dark flower
For you too. That was satisfactory.
Wilder, maybe, than ever Emily knew it.
With wet feet and nothing on her head
She trudged that climbing side towards friends —
Probably. Dark redoubt
On the skyline above. It was all
Novel and exhilarating to you.
The book becoming a map. Wuthering Heights
Withering into perspective. We got there
And it was all gaze. The open moor,
Gamma rays and decomposing starlight
Had repossessed it
With a kind of blackening smoulder. The centuries

Of door-bolted comfort finally amounted
To a forsaken quarry. The roofs'
Deadfall slabs were flaking, but mostly in place,
Beams and purlins softening. So hard
To imagine the life that had lit
Such a sodden, raw-stone cramp of refuge.
The floors were a rubble of stone and sheep droppings.
Doorframes, windowframes —
Gone to make picnickers' fires or evaporated.
Only the stonework — black. The sky — blue.
And the moor-wind flickering.

                       The incomings,
The outgoings — how would you take up now
The clench of that struggle? The leakage
Of earnings off a few sickly bullocks
And a scatter of crazed sheep. Being cornered
Kept folk here. Was that crumble of wall
Remembering a try at a garden? Two trees
Planted for company, for a child to play under,
And to have something to stare at. Sycamores—
The girth and spread of valley twenty-year-olds,
They were probably ninety.

                       You breathed it all in
With jealous, emulous sniffings. Weren't you
Twice as ambitious as Emily? Odd
To watch you, such a brisk pendant
Of your globe-circling aspirations,
Among those burned-out, worn-out remains
Of failed efforts, failed hopes —

Iron beliefs, iron necessities,
Iron bondage, already
Crumbling back to the wild stone.
                            You perched
In one of the two trees
Just where the snapshot shows you.
Doing as Emily never did. You
Had all the liberties, having life.
The future had invested in you —
As you might say of a jewel
So brilliantly faceted, refracting
Every tint, where Emily had stared
Like a dying prisoner. And a poem unfurled from you
Like a loose frond of hair from your nape
To be clipped and kept in a book. What would stern
Dour Emily have made of your frisky glances
And your huge hope? Your huge
Mortgage of hope. The moor-wind
Came with its empty eyes to look at you,
And the clouds gazed sidelong, going elsewhere,
The heath-grass, fidgeting in its fever,
Took idiot notice of you. And the stone,
Reaching to touch your hand, found you real
And warm, and lucent, like that earlier one.
And maybe a ghost, trying to hear your words,
Peered from the broken mullions
And was stilled. Or was suddenly aflame
With the scorch of doubled envy. Only
Gradually quenched in understanding.

Ted Hughes

At Luddenden Foot
August 1840

Like withered hands the first grey sycamore leaves,
Dry-curled, scramble down the deep cutting
on to the stony, steel-bright railway track
as he sits in the tarred wood shed
wasting precious time.
Soon it will be dark, lamps to be lit,
the red signal eye wink down with a crash
to chameleon green;
then on the up line the clanking train
grinds fussily by,
leaving to linger only its wraith-smell
of coal smoke, steam and axle-grease.

Encompassed by the Woodman and the Weavers Arms,
the Irish bargemen and their women,
he will wash all this soot from his lark's throat.
He doodles a demonic face in the marbled ledge;
Heathcliff he names it, then no more.
Instead he turns to a poem,
one to be set beside old Southey's
and so put an ignoring world to rights.

Meanwhile the decrepitating coke stove
emits its sulphur to stab his chest
with an appropriate poniard,
fate posed for treachery.

Lewis Hosegood

Emily also had an aversion to the outside world, preferring to be in the parsonage where she could make herself useful with domestic tasks.

Eventually, Branwell set himself up as a portrait painter in Bradford, where he made friends and received his first commissions. These soon came to an end, however, and he was once again searching for a means of earning a living. In 1840 he took a job as tutor in a family at Broughton, and after this became a railway clerk at Sowerby Bridge. At this time the railway industry was relatively new, and offered a chance of career advancement. From there he went on to become a clerk in charge of Luddendon Foot Station, where he kept ledgers and looked after the station. The work was dull and unsatisfying, and could not occupy his active imagination. Hardly surprisingly, he spent his time scrawling cartoons and fragments of poems over the ledgers. Eventually he was dismissed when a discrepancy was discovered in the accounts. He returned then to the parsonage more miserable then ever, writing to Francis Grundy, a fellow railway clerk:

> '... I only want a motive for exertion to be happier than I
> have been for years. But I feel my recovery from almost
> insanity to be retarded by having nothing to listen to except
> the wind moaning among old chimneys and older ash trees
> and nothing to look at except heathering hills walked over
> when life had all to hope for and nothing to regret with
> me ...'

During this time Branwell had managed to publish some of his work in the *Halifax Guardian*, and his poem *Brearly Hill*, written in August 1841, was the first poem to be published by the Brontë children. It indicates the weary collapsing of Branwell's spirit, as he depicts himself as a man rejected by God.

Brearly Hill

Oh Thou, whose beams were most withdrawn
   When should have risen my morning sun,
Who, frowning most at earliest dawn,
   Foretold the storm through which 't would run;

Great God! when hour on hour has passed
   In an unsmiling storm away,
No sound but bleak December's blast
   No sighs but tempests, through my day.

At length, in twilight's dark decline,
   Roll back the clouds that mark Thy frown,
Give but a single silver line —
   One sunblink, as the day goes down.

My prayer is earnest, for my breast
   No more can buffet with these storms;
I must have one short space of rest
   Ere I go home to dust and worms;

I must a single gleam of light
   Amid increasing darkness see,
Ere I, resigned to churchyard night,
   Bid day farewell eternally!

My body is oppressed with pain,
   My mind is prostrate 'neath despair —
Nor mind nor body may again
   Do more than call Thy wrath to spare,

Both void of power to fight or flee,
   To bear or to avert Thy eye,
With sunken heart, with suppliant knee,
   Implore a peaceful hour to die.

When I look back on former life,
   I scarcely know what I have been
So swift the change from strife to strife
   That passes o'er the wildering scene.

I only feel that every power —
   And Thou hadst given much to me —
Was spent upon the present hour,
   Was never turned, my God, to Thee:

That what I did to make me blest
   Sooner or later changed to pain;
That still I laughed at peace and rest
   So neither must behold again.

Branwell Brontë

THE SISTERS AS GOVERNESSES

As Patrick Brontë lay seriously ill in June 1830 with an inflammation of the lungs, it became increasingly obvious that at some time the children would have to support themselves. In 1831, at the age of fourteen, and financed it is thought by the Reverend Thomas and Mrs Atkinson, her godparents and old friends of her father, Charlotte had enrolled at Roe Head, a small school for young ladies in Dewsbury. At the time the school had only ten boarders. The grounds were large and the situation healthy. With Miss Margaret Wooler as its principal, the school was a happy place where Charlotte received support and companionship.

Although the family was only twenty miles away, without the transport we are used to today it seemed much further and she missed her sisters and brother greatly. Also, Charlotte is thought to have been embarrassed about having to wear glasses. She was very short-sighted and could hardly see without her glasses, presenting herself at first as a lonely and withdrawn figure. Two of the girls at Roe Head, Ellen Nussey and Mary Taylor, befriended her and the three of them were friends for the rest of their lives.

The Old Church Tower

The old church tower and garden wall
Are black with autumn rain.
And dreary winds foreboding call
The darkness down again.

I watched how evening took the place
Of glad and glorious day;
I watched a deeper gloom efface
The evening's lingering ray.

And as I gazed on the cheerless sky
Sad thoughts rose in my mind ...

Emily Brontë

I'll Come When Thou Art Saddest

I'll come when thou art saddest,
Laid alone in the darkened room;
When the mad day's mirth has vanished,
And the smile of joy is banished
From the evening's chilly gloom.

I'll come when the heart's real feeling
Has entire, unbiased sway,
And my influence o'er thee stealing,
Grief deepening, joy congealing,
Shall bear thy soul away.

Listen, 'tis just the hour,
The awful time for thee;
Dost thou not feel upon thy soul
A flood of strange sensations roll,
Forerunners of a sterner power,
Heralds me?

Emily Brontë

Margaret Wooler respected Charlotte's opinion and encouraged her learning through conversation and debate. At Roe Head, Charlotte grew in confidence, and when she left the school, where she had won prizes for her love of poetry, written playlets and ceremonials, she was stronger as a personality and more prepared for life ahead. At first, though, she wanted to pass on some of her learning to her sisters, thinking it might help them support themselves.

In 1835, on the invitation of Miss Wooler, Charlotte returned to Roe Head as a teacher, and as part of her payment she was able to take one of her sisters as a pupil. Emily was seventeen then and accompanied Charlotte.

She did not stay long. The artificial and disciplined lifestyle stifled her, and she longed for home and the freedom of the moors. Charlotte was an important stabilising influence in the family, always restraining her own passion and acting in a maternal role, and writes of Emily:

> '... her white face, attenuated form, and failing strength threatened rapid decline. I felt in my heart she would die, if she did not go home, and with this conviction obtained her recall.'

After Emily went home, Anne, now fifteen, and who we are often led to believe was of a weaker constitution than Emily, joined Charlotte instead. Perhaps her more easy-going nature helped her fit in better, although she too missed the parsonage and her writing. Anne, like Charlotte, had a keen sense of duty and was often a source of both spiritual and physical strength to the family.

A Place for Beginnings

The Red House, Gomersal, Yorkshire.
'Briarmains' in Charlotte Brontë's novel *Shirley*.

Here is a place for beginnings. William Taylor,
who built this house three hundred years ago,
in a land of Yorkshire stone building with brick
— stubbornly different; yet no angler for opinion, no
hankerer after praise or brittle show,
but building as he had to — little guessed
what he had started here

                      The red brick glows
in the evening sun; arboreal shadows press
deeply toward nightfall. Orchard and lawn and house
lie fallow now, remembering what to him
was intention only; what became our heritage;
his future and our past. So we, in turn,
spin different ambitions for an altered age.
He dreamed of family and business and a house
that generations of his blood and name
would home to after journeys. His dream was cloth;
weaving and fulling sheds and the tenter-frame.
Never in all his nights could he figure forth
such a gray-gowned woman, spectacled and small,
who conjured a different dream and, shameless, purloined for it
his trade, his progeny, his nonsuch red-brick walls.
Nor could she dream the changes that have turned
his home into museum, spinning-wheel, loom,
a two-thousand-year-old Celtic head, fossils,
war-relics, Victoriana and a Brontë room!
Sometimes, on an afternoon, I picture her
sheer incredulity, watching her brown eyes show
at first emptiness only, then sudden laughter
and then the pungent wit, the swift bon mot.

78

Mabel Ferrett

The Teacher's Monologue

The room is quiet, thoughts alone
People its mute tranquillity;
The yoke put off, the long task done, —
I am, as it is bliss to be,
Still and untroubled. Now, I see,
For the first time, how soft the day
O'er waveless water, stirless tree,
Silent and sunny, wings its way.
Now, as I watch that distant hill,
So faint, so blue, so far removed,
Sweet dreams of home my heart may fill,
That home where I am known and loved:
It lies beyond; yon azure brow
Parts me from all Earth holds for me;
And, morn and even, my yearnings flow
Thitherward tending, changelessly.
My happiest hours! all the time,
I love to keep in memory,
Lapsed among moors, ere life's first prime
Decayed to dark anxiety.

Sometimes, I think a narrow heart
Makes me thus mourn those far away,
And keeps my love so far apart
From friends and friendships of to-day;
Sometimes, I think 'tis but a dream
I treasure up so jealously,
All the sweet thoughts I live on seem
To vanish into vacancy:
And then, this strange, coarse world around
Seems all that's palpable and true;
And every sight and every sound
Combine my spirit to subdue
To aching grief; so void and lone
Is Life and Earth — so worse than vain,
The hopes that, in my own heart sown,
And cherished by such sun and rain
As joy and transient Sorrow shed,
Have ripened to a harvest there:
Alas! methinks I hear it said,
'Thy golden sheaves are empty air,'
All fades away; my very home
I think will soon be desolate;
I hear, at times, a warning come
Of bitter partings at its gate;
And, if I should return and see
The hearth-fire quenched, the vacant chair;
And hear it whispered mournfully,
That farewells have been spoken there,
What shall I do, and whither turn?
Where look for peace? When cease to mourn?

'Tis not the air I wished to play,
The strain I used to sing;
My wilful spirit slipped away
And struck another string.
I neither wanted smile nor tear,
Bright joy nor bitter woe,
But just a song that sweet and clear,
Though haply sad, might flow.

A quiet song, to solace me
When sleep refused to come;
A strain to chase despondency
When sorrowful for home.
In vain I try; I cannot sing;
All feels so cold and dead;
No wild distress, no gushing spring
Of tears in anguish shed;

But all the impatient gloom of one
Who waits a distant day,
When, some great task of suffering done,
Repose shall toil repay.
For youth departs, and pleasure flies,
And life consumes away,
And youth's rejoicing ardour dies
Beneath this drear delay;

And Patience, weary with her yoke,
Is yielding to despair,
And Health's elastic spring is broke
Beneath the strain of care.
Life will be gone ere I have lived;
Where now is Life's first prime?
I've worked and studied, longed and grieved,
Through all that rosy time.

To toil, to think, to long, to grieve ——
Is such my future fate?
The morn was dreary, must the eve
Be also desolate?

Well, such a life at least makes Death
A welcome, wished-for friend;
Then, aid me, Reason, Patience, Faith,
To suffer to the end!

Charlotte Brontë

Ellen Nussey Observes

Charlotte is painting my portrait.
(I think there is nothing she cannot do!)
'Dear Nell', says she, 'your eyes wander over much.
Beware Mr Weightman's attentions. I fear he's a satyr,
dances and sings at the least provocation,
leaps tussocks, balances on field walls,
bringing hot flushes to our little Anne
who's scarce out of the schoolroom.
Nor is he above ogling between sermons
half the lasses of Haworth.'
Anne is struggling with German.
(I think there is nothing she will not attempt).
'Was hast du gestern gelesen?'
she demands of a mournful cow
who unsurprisingly answers her not.
She means to discuss Goethe with Emmy.
In a moment the two will go off together,
lie on the sward of this brief summer,
chew grass stalks and smell the earth
which is already in love with them both.

Lewis Hosegood

When Emily came back to the parsonage from Roe Head, the atmosphere must have been very sad and depressing, and it is difficult not to wonder at the workings of the family praxis and other reasons for Emily's return. The children were so much part and parcel of each other, sometimes it is difficult to know where one ends and another begins, or where they flow into each other's work: Branwell is Heathcliff — is Rochester — is Emily? 'I *am* Heathcliff!' Catherine says in *Wuthering Heights*. And is she?

Anne had gone to Roe Head, and Branwell was in a state of shock and disillusionment. Whilst a gifted painter, he had never really loved the work in the way he loved writing. But he was highly gifted in many ways, perhaps too gifted, in that his impulsive nature and the pressure he may have felt to find the right path may have resulted in considerable confusion as to which way he should go.

The Roe Head school had moved by Easter 1837 to Mirfield Moor so that Miss Wooler could be near her ageing parents. She was also thinking about retiring, and gave Charlotte more responsibility in the school. Charlotte's payment was, however, meagre and she despaired of ever being able to save anything. She too suffered from acute home-sickness, and missed the stimulating and loving companionship of her family.

Parting

There's no use in weeping,
Though we are condemned to part;
There's such a thing as keeping
A remembrance in one's heart:

There's such a thing as dwelling
On the thought ourselves have nursed,
And with scorn and courage telling
The world to do its worse.

We'll not let its follies grieve us,
We'll just take them as they come;
And then every day will leave us
A merry laugh for home.

When we've left each friend and brother,
When we're parted, wide and far,
We will think of one another,
As even better than we are.

Every glorious sight above us,
Every pleasant sight beneath,
We'll connect with those that love us,
Whom we truly love till death!

In the evening, when we're sitting
By the fire, perchance alone,
Then shall heart with warm heart meeting,
Give responsive tone for tone.

We can burst the bonds which chain us,
Which cold human handshake wrought,
And where none shall dare restrain us
We can meet again, in thought.

So there's no use in weeping —
Bear a cheerful spirit still:
Never doubt that Fate is keeping
Future good for present ill!

Charlotte Brontë

Both Branwell and Charlotte sought advice about their writing, Charlotte sending some of her poems to Southey, the then Poet Laureate, who replied:

'Literature cannot be the business of a woman's life, and it ought not to be. The more she is engaged in her proper duties, the less leisure she will have for it, even as an accomplishment and a recreation.'

Southey's letter was discouraging, and at first Charlotte felt ashamed that she had troubled him in such a way. But on re-reading his letter several times she realised that Southey was not condemning her poetry out of hand. He thought that Charlotte had poetic ability 'in no inconsiderable degree, but felt that her daydreaming was peculiar. Charlotte wrote to him again:

'You do not forbid me to write; you do not say that what I write is utterly destitute of merit. You only warn me against the folly of neglecting real duties for the sake of imaginative pleasures; of writing for the love of fame; for the selfish excitement of emulation. You kindly allow me to write poetry for its own sake, provided I have undone nothing which I ought to do, in order to pursue that single, absorbing, exquisite gratification. I am afraid, sir, you think me very foolish. I know the first letter I wrote to you was all senseless trash from beginning to end; but I am not altogether the idle, dreaming being it would seem to denote'.

Southey was more friendly in his next communication, signing himself her 'sincere friend'.

Charlotte and Anne had tried to reconcile themselves to being governesses, although both of them hated teaching. Charlotte writes:

'I am miserable when I allow myself to dwell on the necessity of spending my life as a governess ...'

But Charlotte had trained herself to bend inclination to duty. She writes on the 4th May 1841 from Upperwood House in Rawdon, where she worked with the White family:

'Somehow, I have managed to get a good deal more control over the children lately — this makes my life a good deal easier; also by dint of nursing the fat baby, it has got to know me and be fond of me. I suspect myself of growing rather fond of it.'

Looking for Heathcliff

Today the moor was drenched in cloud,
My gown weighed heavy.
All I could see was wind-scoured
Rock and heather. I searched
For the tracks of his horse,
Felt at the back of caves
For empty wine-skins.

Tonight by the parlour fire
My sister is attentive to the curate,
Who stuffs his smooth pink cheeks
With seed-cake as he chatters.
His fish eyes gleam
But not, I fear, for my sister
Who has told me that she thinks
That she may love him.

On the moor —
He's riding.
The wind that rocks our chimney
Rushes through his hair.
If I draw aside the curtain
I will see how the cloud has lifted;
How under a great white moon
He gallops across the skyline
On his bold black mare —
His body
Close upon her withers
As she beats against the tempest.

Frances Nagle

Emily Brontë

All is the same still. Earth and heaven locked in
A wrestling dream the seasons cannot break;
Shrill the wind tormenting my obdurate thorn trees,
Moss-rose and stone-chat silent in its wake,
Time has not altered here the rhythms I was rocked in,
Creation's throb and ache.

All is yet the same, for mine was a country
Stoic, unregenerate, beyond the power
Of man to mollify or God to disburden —
An ingrown landscape none might long endure
But one who could meet with a passion wilder-wintry
The scalding breath of the moor.

All is yet the same as when I roved the heather
Chained to a demon through the shrieking night,
Took him by the throat while he flailed my sibylline
Assenting breast, and won him to delight.
O truth and pain immortally bound together!
O lamp the storm made bright!

Still on those heights prophetic winds are raving,
Heath and harebell intone a plainsong grief;
'Shrink, soul of man, shrink into your valleys —
Too sharp that agony, that spring too brief!
Love, though your love is but the forged engraving
Of hope on a stricken leaf!'

Is there one whom blizzards warm and rains enkindle
And the bitterest furnace could not more refine?
Anywhere one too proud for consolation,
Burning for pure freedom so that he will pine,
Yes, to the grave without her? Let him mingle
His barren dust with mine.

But is there one who faithfully has planted
His seed of light in the heart's deepest scar?
When the night is darkest, when the wind is keenest,
He, shall find upclimbing from afar
Over his pain my chaste, my disenchanted
And death-rebuking star.

Cecil Day-Lewis

But the horrors of being a governess continued to haunt Charlotte, and she sympathised with others who were trapped in the same service. Anne fared surprisingly well, remaining with the same family, the Robinsons of Thorp Green Hall near York, for five years, for which she received Charlotte's great admiration. Something else, however, was to disturb Anne's quiet at this time. This was the arrival of William Weightman, her father's new curate, a jovial and flirtatious fellow who brought sparkle and fresh air into their lives and endeared himself to everybody. For some reason the Brontë sisters christened him 'Miss Celia Amelia', and always referred to him by this name. Tragically, Weightman was to die in a cholera epidemic at the age of twenty-eight whilst himself attending the sick of Haworth parish. He was buried by Patrick, who, at the funeral, praising Weightman's life said:

> 'In his preaching, and practising, he was, as every clergyman ought to be, neither too distant nor austere, timid nor obtrusive, not bigoted, exclusive nor dogmatical. He was affable but not familiar; open, but not too confusing. He thought it better, and more scriptural, to make the love of God, rather than the fear of Hell, the ruling motive for obedience.'

Charlotte notes of his relationship with Anne:

> 'He sits opposite Anne at Church, sighing softly and looking out of the corners of his eyes to win her attention — and Anne is so quiet, her look so downcast — they are a picture.'

On learning that none of the sisters had ever received a valentine, Weightman walked ten miles to Bradford to send them a poem each. Charlotte, who did not normally like her father's curates, thought him 'bonny, pleasant, light-hearted, good-tempered, generous, careless, fickle and unclerical'.

Night

I love the silent hour of night,
    For blissful dreams may then arise,
Revealing to my charmed sight
    What may not bless my waking eyes.

And then a voice may meet my ear
    That death has silenced long ago;
And hope and rapture may appear
    Instead of solitude and woe.

Cold in the grave for years has lain
    The form it was my bliss to see;
And only dreams can bring again
    The darling of my heart to me.

Anne Brontë

Yes Thou Art Gone

Yes thou art gone! and never more
  Thy sunny smile shall gladden me;
But I may pass the old church door,
  And pace the floor that covers thee,

May stand upon the cold, damp stone,
  And think that, frozen, lies below
The lightest heart that I have known,
  The kindest I shall ever know.

Yet, though I cannot see thee more,
  'Tis still a comfort to have seen;
And though thy transient life is o'er,
  'Tis sweet to think that thou has been;

To think a soul so near divine,
  Within a form so angel fair,
United to a heart like thine,
  Has gladdened once our humble sphere.

Anne Brontë

Severed and Gone

Ah no! thy spirit lingers still
    Where'er thy sunny smile was seen;
There's less of darkness, less of chill
    On earth than if thou had'st not been.

Thou breathest in my bosom yet,
    And dwellest in my beating heart;
And while I cannot quite forget,
    Thou, darling, can'st not quite depart.

Life seems more sweet that thou did'st live,
    And men more true that thou wert one;
Nothing is lost that thou did'st give,
    Nothing destroyed that thou has done.

Anne Brontë

A Valentine

A Combined Effort for William Weightman

A Roland for your Oliver
    We think you've justly earned;
You sent us such a valentine;
    Your gift is now returned.

We cannot write or talk like you;
    We're plain folks every one;
You've played a clever jest on us,
    We thank you for the fun.

Believe us when we frankly say
    (Our words, though blunt, are true),
At home, abroad, by night or day,
    We all wish well to you.

And never may a cloud come o'er
    The sunshine of your mind;
Kind friends, warm hearts, and happy hours
    Through life, we trust, you'll find.

Wher'er you go, however far
    In future years you stray,
There shall not want our earnest prayer
    To speed you on your way.

A stranger and a pilgrim here
    We know you sojourn now;
But brighter hopes, with brighter wreaths,
    Are doomed to bind your brow.

Not always in these lonely hills
    Your humble lot shall lie;
The oracle of fate foretells
    A worthier destiny.

And though her words are veiled in gloom,
    Though clouded her decree,
Yet doubt not that a juster doom
    She keeps in store for thee.

Then cast hope's anchor near the shore,
    'Twill hold your vessel fast,
And fear not for the tide's deep roar,
    And dread not for the blast.

For thought this station now seems near,
    'Mid land-locked creeks to be,
The helmsman soon his ship will steer
    Out to the wide blue sea.

Well officered and staunchly manned,
    Well built to meet the blast;
With favouring winds the bark must land
    On glorious shores at last.

The Brontë Sisters

94

Emily

On these high and solitary moors
crossed with drystone walls,
purple in autumn, snowlocked in winter
she walked, breathed in mysteries
seeded them in imagination.

Being a parsonage child then
freed the girl from the loom's clatter,
from the chattering energy of the demon progress.
She strove to create wild tales,
wove an intricate and coloured web
of another, imagined world.

They said she made bread, read poems,
heard the servant's tale of ghosts and ghouls.
Listened to the hidden ghost within.
Later in stone-flagged house
she laboured to birth immortal poems
by candle and smoking firelight.

Now on these lonely moors where curlews rise —
high and proud in solitude —
her spirit walks, touches mine, and flies.

Jean Barker

BRUSSELS

During the time that had preceded the death of William Weightman, the sisters, Aunt Branwell and Patrick Brontë had been discussing the idea of opening a school, as the Wooler sisters had done. Aunt Branwell offered to support the venture using her own money. At this time, Mary Taylor had gone to Brussels with her brother, writing exciting letters to Charlotte, telling her about the place.

'I hardly know what swelled to my throat as I read her letters', Charlotte writes. She had come to realise the parochial nature of her life, and longed to exercise her talents and experience in other places. She saw going to 'finishing school' as a way of preparing herself for the starting of their school, and wrote to Aunt Branwell from Rawdon, where she was employed as a governess, outlining her plan. The time abroad, she said, would serve to enlighten and prepare her for what she wanted to do:

> *'I feel certain, while I am writing, that you will see the propriety of what I say; you always like to use your money to the best advantage, you are not fond of making shabby purchases; when you do confer a favour, it is often done in style; and depend on it, £50 or £100 thus laid out would be well-employed. Of course, I know no other in the*

world to whom I could apply on this subject except yourself. I feel an absolute conviction that, if this advantage were allowed us, it would be the making of us for life'.

Charlotte then went on to remind her aunt of the way her father had also been ambitious and had left Ireland to go to Cambridge University.

The money Charlotte requested was a substantial sum in those days, and Aunt Branwell showed her extreme generosity by coming to their aid so that plans could be set in motion.

Charlotte was to go as as student to Brussels, to the Pensionnat Heger in Rue d'Isabelle under the supervision of Monsieur Heger, aged thirty-three, and his wife, who was thirty-eight. Emily was to join Charlotte at the school.

Their father Patrick accompanied them, and stayed with them in London at the Chapter Coffee House, where he had stayed at the time of his ordination.

Charlotte and Emily soon found they were the only Protestants in the Catholic school, although Charlotte was happy there, the role of student suiting her better than that of governess. Heger was an excellent teacher and ran the school as a family affair with comfortable domestic arrangements.

There followed an infatuation on Charlotte's part for Monsieur Heger, who was a handsome and clever man. This was to last for many years and is recreated in *The Professor* in the same way that Cowan Bridge was recreated in *Jane Eyre*.

In The Brontë Museum, Haworth

No dull catalogue this.
Their lives leap from the rooms
of the parsonage as Heathcliff
and Rochester from the page.

Emily's German Grammar propped
for study on the table where she made bread.
Charlotte's writing box, her glasses,
letters to editors, firm man's hand.

Dates of deaths too grim
to contemplate. Charlotte's loss
in eighteen months of Emily, Branwell,
Anne, emblematic in the view;
from every room the bleak graveyard;
church squat against winds.
And beyond, the moor, rolling outwards
but enclosing inwards.

In her bedroom, filled with displays
of bonnets, collars, dainty gloves,
all Charlotte's, I stand beside the central
showcase and a dummy her size

in silk dress almost rustling next to me.
With a shiver, shoulder to shoulder
I see it is my height … Neat, small …
The boots made for me.

Sally Carr

Three

Three silent women at the kitchen table.
My mother's kitchen is dark and small but out of the window
there is the moor, paralyzed with ice.
It extends as far as the eye can see

over flat miles to a solid unlit white sky.
Mother and I are chewing lettuce carefully.
The kitchen wall clock emits a ragged low buzz that jumps

once a minute over the twelve.
I have Emily p216 propped upon the sugarbowl
but am covertly watching my mother.

A thousand questions hit my eyes from inside.
My mother is studying her lettuce.
I turn to p217

'In my flight through the kitchen I knocked over Hareton
who was hanging a litter of puppies
from a chairback in the doorway ... '

It is as if we have all been lowered into an atmosphere of glass.
Now and then a remark trails through the glass.
Taxes on the back lot. Not a good melon,

too early for melons.
Hairdresser in two found God, closes shop every Tuesday.
Mice in the tea-towel drawer again.
Little pellets. Chew off

the corners of the napkins, if they knew
what paper napkins cost nowadays.
Rain tonight.

Rain tomorrow.
That volcano in the Philippines at it again. What's her name
Anderson died no not Shirley

the opera singer. Negress.
Cancer.
Not eating your garnish, you don't like pimento?

Out of the window I can see dead leaves ticking over the flatland
and dregs of snow scarred by pine filth.
At the middle of the moor

where the ground goes down into a depression,
the ice has begun to unclench.
Black open water comes

curdling up like anger. My mother speaks suddenly.
That psycotherapy's not doing you much good is it?
You aren't getting over him.

My mother has a way of summing things up.
She never liked Law much
but she liked the idea of me having a man and getting on with life

Well he's a taker and you're a giver I hope it works out,
was all she said after she met him.
Give and take were just words to me

at the time. I had not been in love before.
It was like a wheel rolling downhill.
But early this morning while mother slept

and I was downstairs reading the part in Wuthering Heights
where Heathcliff clings at the lattice in the storm sobbing
Come in! Come in! to the ghost of his heart's darling.

Dogs and Bread

Emily Brontë is making bread,
she digs the heel of her hand
into the six-pound batch of dough,
Rhythmically and studies her German.
When father's eyes fail
she discharges the gun every morning.

Also she looks after the dogs,
fearsome, square-headed,
they know she will beat them with fists
if she has to. She feeds them
on the eye of death
walking slowly
with the broken meats held in her apron.

She does not care for your opinion
of what she wrote or how she lived.
The risen bread is lifting the cloth.

Annie Foster

I fell on my knees on the rug and sobbed too.
She knows how to hang puppies,
that Emily.

It isn't like taking an aspirin you know, I answer feebly.
Dr Haw says grief is a long process.
She frowns. What does it accomplish

all that raking up the past?
Oh — I spread my hands —
I prevail! I look her in the eye.
She grins. Yes you do.

Anne Carson, from *The Glass Essay*

Patrick Brontë

(Patrick Brontë's spectacles are preserved
in the Brontë Museum, Haworth)

From Patrick Brontë's bedroom window —
  graves,
from daughter Charlotte's bedroom window —
  graves,
from children's study and servants' bedroom —
  graves.

Young, he had run barefoot
helping his father in flat fields,
observed blue distant mountains;
taught himself to read and write,
visions ascending to those blue tops.

Now in his graveyard house
  his spectacles
museum-preserved, tinted blue —
still reaching towards the sky.

Mary Hodgson

Emily, although benefiting academically from her stay in Brussels, longed for home. At this time, Branwell was to write:

> 'I have had long attendance at the death-bed of the Reverend William Weightman, one of my dearest friends, and now I am attending at the death of my aunt, who has been for twenty years as a mother.'

Aunt Branwell had developed a blockage in the stomach, Branwell having to witness 'such agonising suffering as I would not wish my worse enemy to endure'. Their aunt was to die and be buried by the time the girls arrived home. She had left each of them a small income and various effects:

> 'Should I die at Haworth, I request that my remains may be deposited in the church in that place as near as convenient to the remains of my dear sister … My Indian workbox, I leave to my niece, Charlotte Brontë; my workbox with a china top I leave to my niece Emily Jane Brontë together with my ivory fan; my Japan dressing box I leave to my nephew, Patrick Branwell Brontë; to my niece Anne Brontë, I leave my watch with all that belongs with it; as also my eyeglass and its chain, my rings, silver spoons, books, clothes etc etc I leave to be divided between my above named three nieces …'

Emily was to stay behind at the parsonage to take care of the domestic arrangements, whilst Charlotte returned to Madame Heger's school. Both Charlotte and Emily had been invited to become teachers at the school, whilst Anne stayed with the Robinson family at Thorp Green. As part of her work Charlotte was to teach Heger English, a task she enjoyed, since she had become deeply attached to the man. However, Madame Heger was to discover this and set about arranging it so that Charlotte and her husband had less time together. This caused Charlotte to again feel lonely and isolated, and she wrote to Emily and Branwell in October 1843 of her need for companionship:

> 'Dear E J — This Sunday morning. They are at their idolatrous masse, and I am here — … tell me whether Papa really wants me

very much to come home, and whether you do like-wise. I have an idea that I should be of no use there — a sort of aged person upon the parish. I pray, with heart and soul, that all may continue well at Haworth; above all in our grey, half-inhabited house. God bless the walls thereof!'

Charlotte was becoming increasingly unhappy in Brussels, imagining the others were discussing and spying on her. In December 1843 she wrote to Emily requesting money to assist her return home. Heger had promised to correspond with her, although many of her letters later remained unanswered, whilst she wrote from her heart in deep despair at being deprived of the 'friendship' of her 'master'.

By this time Patrick Brontë was becoming old and frail, and his eyesight had begun to deteriorate badly, so that he depended heavily upon his curates. The new curate at this time, Arthur Bell Nicholls, was hardworking and had a generous heart. After a complicated courtship, he and Charlotte were eventually to marry.

Since arriving in Haworth, Patrick Brontë had built the Sunday schools, and installed an organ and bells at the church. Also two new churches were to serve parts within the parish outside the village: the small mission church at Stanbury, and St Mary's at Oxenhope. Patrick had involved himself in all public affairs, writing to newspapers, making outspoken attacks on the new Poor Law Act and other political happenings of the day, both in print and orally at public gatherings.

from *Reason*

Unloved I love, unwept I weep,
Grief I restrain, hope I repress;
Vain is this anguish, fixed and deep,
Vainer desires or means of bliss.

My life is cold, love's fire being dead;
That fire self-kindled, self-consumed;
What living warmth erewhile it shed,
Now to how drear extinction doomed!

Devoid of charm how could I dream
My unasked love would e'er return?
What fate, what influence lit the flame
I still feel inly, deeply burn?

Alas! there are those who should not love;
I to this dreary band belong;
This knowing let me henceforth prove
Too wise to list delusions's song.

Charlotte Brontë

He Saw My Heart's Woe

He saw my heart's woe, discovered my soul's anguish,
How in fever, in thirst, in atrophy it pines;
Knew he could heal, yet looked and let it languish,
To its moans spirit-deaf, to its pangs spirit-blind.

But once a year he heard a whisper low and dreary
Appealing for aid, entreating some reply;
Only when sick, soul-worn, and torture-weary,
Breathed I that prayer, heaved I that sigh.

He was mute as is the grave, he stood stirless as a tower;
At last I looked up, and saw I prayed to stone;
I asked help of that which to help had no power,
I sought love where love was utterly unknown.

Idolator I kneeled to an idol cut in rock!
I might have slashed my flesh and drawn my heart's best blood:
The Granite God had felt no tenderness, no shock;
My Baal had not seen nor heard nor understood.

In dark remorse I rose: I rose in darker shame;
Self-condemned I withdrew to an exile from my kind;

A solitude I sought where mortal never came,
Hoping in its wilds forgetfulness to find,
Now, Heaven, heal the wound which I still deeply feel;
Thy glorious hosts look not in scorn on our poor race;
Thy King eternal doth no iron judgement deal
On suffering worms who seek forgiveness, comfort, grace.

He gave our hearts to love: He will not Love despise,
E'en if the gift be lost, as mine was long ago;
He will forgive the fault, will bid the offender rise,
Wash out with dews of bliss the fiery brand of woe;

And give a sheltered place beneath the unsullied throne,
Whence the soul redeemed may mark Time's fleeting course
    round earth;
And know its trials overpast, its sufferings gone,
And feel the peril past of Death's immortal birth.

Charlotte Brontë

THE NOVELS AND BRANWELL'S DECLINE

Home thoughts are not with me,
Bright as of yore.
Joys are forgot by me,
Taught to deplore.

Branwell Brontë

Branwell had been working as tutor to Edmund Robinson at Thorp Green Hall, a large house surrounded by trees, two and a half miles from the village of Little Ouseburn and twelve from York, whilst Charlotte was in Brussels, and had, it seemed, been very successful. Some time after Charlotte returned home from Brussels, Branwell was dismissed, receiving a note from Mr Robinson to the effect that his 'proceedings, had been bad beyond expression'. He was to cut off all communication with every member of the Robinson family.

In a letter to J B Leyland, Branwell tells him that he and Lydia, wife of Mr Robinson, had felt more than friendship for each other in that she had shown him 'a degree of kindness which, when I was deeply grieved one day at her husband's conduct, ripened into declarations of more than ordinary feelings ... '

New evidence now points to Branwell having had an affair with Lydia Robinson. He became very depressed, and that, along with Charlotte's grief at having to leave Monsieur Heger, made the parsonage a solemn and unhappy place at this time.

Branwell fell into deeper and deeper despair, resorting to drugs and gradually wasting away, making grotesque drawings of himself and demonic creatures so that he could hardly tell truth from nightmare. 'The poor man does what he can', he says of his father.

Various accounts are given of the state of Lydia Robinson's mind after her husband had died. A letter sent from the Robinson's family solicitor is said to have 'stunned' Branwell 'into marble'. She had apparently 'stared' at the doctor and 'fainted' at the mention of Branwell's name. There had been talk of her entering a nunnery. Branwell writes to Leyland:

> ' … if I sit down and try to write, all ideas that used to come
> clothed in sunlight now press round me in funeral black … '

The idea the sisters had cherished of having their own school had now come to nothing. They had drawn up a prospectus and advertised, but no one had enquired.

Increasingly they took to their writing, attempting at the same time to cope with Branwell's frantic behaviour as best they could. Anne had returned from Thorp Green after witnessing 'some very unpleasant and undreamt of experience of human nature'.

In these very sombre moments of the Brontë's history, all the inhabitants of the household had to find a way of surviving. Still taking care of the domestic arrangements, Anne also wrote about her religious beliefs. Emily spent much of her time looking after Branwell, and also writing. Charlotte wrote later about finding some of Emily's poetry:

> 'One day, in the autumn of 1845, I accidentally lighted on an
> MS volume of my sister Emily's handwriting. Of course I was not
> surprised, knowing that she could and did write verse. I looked it
> over, and something more than surprise seized me — a deep
> conviction that these were no common effusions, not at all like the
> poetry women generally write'.

Emily was essentially a very private person, and Charlotte's disclosure caused a greater degree of anger than she could have ever imagined. However, she was convinced that Emily's poetry should be published and available to the world, and waited until her sister came round to her way of thinking. Eventually Emily was persuaded, and the poems were put together with Charlotte's and some of Anne's, who now brought forward those of her own. Together the three sisters decided to seek publication.

Emily

Imagine a poet
    verse-forced to show
    those secret words
    before their time.
Imagine her sister
    quietly offering
    sweet rhymes,
    unchallenging sincerity.
Imagine the author
    whose prose breathed life
    where poetry
    would not form.
Imagine the poet,
    and forget diaries, novels,
    letters: find truth
    in literature's height.

Alison Chisholm

Jane

'Would Miss *Jane Eyre* please report to Airport Information.
Miss *Jane Eyre*, please'. — heard over PA at Heathrow

and he thrust himself into the streams
from every continent — a salmon
shouldering, winding,
searching for a face as pale as chalk.
A bookstore! Surely she'd be there,
peering at the print of worlds she recognised?
No. Nor in the transit lounge
with massive Asian families,
nor the Ladies, weeping beneath
the mounting roar of jets and air-conditioning.
He leaps the stairs — she may be taking
a demure, if plastic, cup of tea —
and surveys the concourse. A dark
hooded bird of prey, he sifts, sifts
the dress of all the nations
for a frock in English grey.
Would he catch her tiny voice
in this damned babble?
The information desk — she shakes her head.
'Shall I page again, Sir?'
He gives a brusque 'No. It was an
off-chance, just an off-chance'.
'Is the lady departing or arriving, Sir,
from where?' But he's striding
from the terminal, and minutes later,
his land rover nudges the northbound carriageway.

Kathleen Jamie

Lines Written at Thorp Green

That summer sun, whose genial glow
Now cheers my drooping spirit so,
Must cold and silent be,
And only light our northern clime
With feeble ray, before the time
I long so much to see.

And this soft, whispering breeze, that now
So gently cools my fevered brow,
This too, alas! must turn
To a wild blast, whose icy dart
Pierces and chills me to the heart,
Before I cease to mourn.

And these bright flowers I love so well,
Verbena, rose, and sweet bluebell,
Must droop and die away;
Those thick, green leaves, with all their shade
And rustling music, they must fade,
And everyone decay.

But if the sunny, summer time,
And woods and meadows in their prime,
Are sweet to them that roam;
Far sweeter is the winter bare,
With long, dark nights, and landscape drear,
To them that are at Home!

Anne Brontë

The Brontë Brother

I hear them at night whispering
In their odorous and dark sisterhood,
'How will we get away?' Amid the comfort

Of their shared bed, the moonlight
Making beautiful African hills of the bedclothes,
Their hair seems sewn to their heads,

The beautiful stitching that divides their hair
With such a straight white line,
Their scalps are so pale.

When I see the crowns of their heads on the pillow
It is three faint white lines each at an angle
To the other like half-formed lettering.

And one fears she will be the last to die,
And one uses her clothes
As a feathery shadow. (I lie

In the moonlight in the garden
And I play with the light to see
If I can feel it with my eyes shut

Moving my hand smoothly from shadow to light
And when I feel the moon's heat I open my eyes
And see this exquisite blue candelabra

Hanging in the dark garden air).
And I imagine them in jewels and metal necklaces
As though an oval mirror had been

Broken over them and they wore its fragments
As acts of Heroism.
And I will be drunk on moonlight

As I watch their safe sleep
And the strong smell of their young hair
And their paper white scalps.

My breath passes in clouds over them.
One day I will do a picture of them,
Without their hands, of course,

And I will fold my painting over
So that the future will make
a ghost cross, a faint cross

Across the face of the painting,
A flaking cross of missing paint
Like the beautiful seams of their heads

That the future will unfold my sisters
As they watch moonlight through a window frame
And see them as bearers of an invisible cross.

Gerard Woodward

The financing of the publishing was to come from money Aunt Branwell had left them, and the poems were eventually published by Aylott and Jones of London under the pseudonyms of Currer, Ellis and Acton Bell, coming out in a small blue volume in May 1846. Only two copies were sold, but the Brontës believed in themselves and knew their brilliance. They were not discouraged. Charlotte writes:

'Ill-success failed to crush us; the mere effort to succeed had given a wonderful zest to existence … We each set to work on a prose tale'.
It is thought that all this activity was kept from Branwell, who was still deeply disturbed and physically ill. Patrick's eyesight grew worse, and Charlotte had to take him to Manchester to see Dr William James Wilson MRCS, who was honorary surgeon at the Manchester Infirmary. Patrick's eye needed operating on for a cataract, and this was done on the 25th August without an anaesthetic whilst Charlotte comforted him by holding his hand. She wrote that her father had 'displayed extraordinary patience and firmness; the surgeons seemed surprised'.

The operation was successful, and Patrick began to read again and write and find his way about. Whilst his eyes were bandaged and he was convalescing, Charlotte had developed a severe toothache, and in order to distract herself, she set about writing a story. This was to be her great masterpiece *Jane Eyre*.

Later on that year, Patrick was conducting Sunday services again, and throughout this time Emily and Anne had been taking care of Branwell. In the evenings the girls walked round the parlour arm in arm, discussing their writing in the manner Charlotte had adopted from Roe Head where Miss Wooler would walk in the evening, a girl on each arm, discussing the day's work.

The prose manuscripts were sent from publisher to publisher whilst the true identity of the 'Bells' was kept secret. Eventually, in August 1846, *Wuthering Heights* and *Agnes Grey* were accepted, provided some of the cost was borne by the authors themselves. Charlotte's own work, *The Professor*, was rejected.

Mourning Ring

Jane Eyre Chapter 27

Does sunrise splash the swallow's breast
as brightly now? —
and is that hare
sniffing the wind
on the grey crested hill,
as ignorant as was she
that the despoiler comes
to raid each paradise?

Mourning and morning
they are the same to her
in meaning as in sound,
and can she now believe
that ring had lain so close,
till twelve calm words
uttered in formal tones
came like a magpie's theft.

Swallows and hares
birds in each brake and copse
are true to their loves;
but she
will not glance
at what is left behind,
dares not look
at the future's form,
cannot see
where through a darkened wood
lies a colossal head
with hollow eyes.
And what's beyond —
a pilgrimage — eternal — without shrine? —
perhaps a blinding hell —
or fragile heaven?

Ian Emberson

The Consolation

Though bleak these woods, and damp
   the ground
With fallen leaves so thickly strown,
And cold the wind that wanders round
With wild and melancholy moan;

There is a friendly roof I know,
Might shield me from the wintry blast;
There is a fire, whose ruddy glow
Will cheer me for my wanderings past.

And so, though still, where'er I go,
Cold stranger-glances meet my eye;
Though, when my spirit sinks in woe,
Unheeded swells the unbidden sigh;

Though solitude, endured too long,
Bids youthful joys too soon decay,
Makes mirth a stranger to my tongue,
And overclouds my noon of day;

When kindly thoughts that would have way,
Flow back discouraged to my breast;
I know there is, though far away,
A home where heart and soul may rest.

Warm hands are there, that, clasped in mind,
The warmer heart will not belie;
While mirth, and truth, and friendship shine
In smiling lip and earnest eye.

The ice that gathers round my heart
May there be thawed; and sweetly, then,
The joys of youth, that now depart,
Will come to cheer my soul again.

Though far I roam, that thought shall be
My hope, my comfort, everywhere;
While such a home remains to me,
My heart shall never know despair.

Anne Brontë

Home

How brightly glistening in the sun
  The woodland ivy plays!
While yonder beeches from their barks
  Reflect his silver rays.

That sun surveys a lovely scene
  From softly smiling skies;
And wildly through unnumbered trees
  The wind of winter sighs:

Now loud, it thunders o'er my head,
  And now in distance dies.
But give me back by barren hills
  Where colder breezes rise;

Where scarce the scattered, stunted trees
  Can yield an answering swell,
But where a wilderness of heath
  Returns the sound as well.

For yonder garden, fair and wide,
  With groves of evergreen,
Long winding walks, and borders trim,
  And velvet lawns between —

Restore to me that little spot,
  With grey walls compassed round,
Where knotted grass neglected lies,
  And weeds usurp the ground.

Though all around this mansion high
  Invites the foot to roam,
And though its halls are fair within —
  Oh, give me back my HOME!

Anne Brontë

Wuthering Heights

The horizons ring me like faggots,
Tilted and disparate, and always unstable.
Touched by a match, they might warm me,
And their fine lines singe
The air to orange
Before the distances they pin evaporate,
Weighting the pale sky with a solider colour.
But they only dissolve and dissolve
Like a series of promises, as I step forward.

There is no life higher than the grasstops
Or the hearts of sheep, and the wind
Pours by like destiny, bending
Everything in one direction.
I can feel it trying
To funnel my heat away.
If I pay the roots of the heather
Too close attention, they will invite me
To whiten my bones among them.

The sheep know where they are,
Browsing in their dirty wool-clouds,
Gray as the weather.
The black slots of their pupils take me in.
It is like being mailed into space,
A thin, silly message.
They stand about in grandmotherly disguise,
All wig curls and yellow teeth
Sand hard, marbly baas.

I come to wheel ruts, and water
Limpid as the solitude
That flee through my fingers.
Hollow doorsteps go from grass to grass;
Lintel and sill have unhinged themselves.
Of people the air only
Remembers a few odd syllables.
It rehearses them moaningly:
Black stone, black stone.

The sky leans on me, me, the one upright
Among all horizontals.
The grass is beating its head distractedly.
It is too delicate
For a life in such company;
Darkness terrifies it.
Now in valleys narrow
And black as purses, the house lights
Gleam like small change.

Sylvia Plath

Branwell

It must have been like living with the Three Graces
there on that Yorkshire moor
for Branwell: his paintpot, beer and braces,
secret thoughts of a wench
in Leeds or Liverpool or Manchester.

'Tha's a lot o' genius lad!' it's said
his dad encouraged him with,
and constant as a brutal refrain
the words ran through his head.

An austere father whose presence brooded over
the cold parsonage: not unkindly
but he maybe favoured the girls,
the feminine's paternal lover

they being 'the apples of his eyes'?
Yet another variant of the Eden thing
Branwell concluded early
in jealousy, first of Emily the wise

then, later, of the other two: shrill
Charlotte, 'whose romantic appeal suited ill with . . . ?'
but he could never finish the thought or get used
to those attacks of ill-will

on his part — even once having mauled
timorous Anne verbally in childhood,
and all because she'd said 'summut and nowt'
about what? That he could not recall appalled

him as much as would have the day they laid
his 'timorous Anne' in Scarborough's churchyard
when, had he been there, although an atheist
he would surely have prayed?

Eventually, though, he lost himself in laudanum,
meaningless kisses and grief,
trying his hand at this and that to get on
in the world of art, but dogged by the belief
that genius like love had been unfairly shared
in that parsonage of brass and luck and the noise of bibles.

William Oxley

Branwell Speaks

Night. The visitors are gone ...

Around our square haunted table
my sisters all three sit
scribbling their foolish fantasies,
unheeding the fall of white hearth-coals
before which Keeper sprawls, stirs
and occasionally farts in his sleep.
Scratchety-scratch whisper all three pens,
Till all three hands reach out at once
for the square glass inkwell on the red chenille.

Tock and slowly tock
intones the long-dead clock
as the wind this wild December
blows coldly down from Top Withens.
My father's in his room
which faces his monolith of a church
dark grey-green there in the snowlight
to exorcise the howl of the moor.
All, all are at work, all except me.
I hunch in my chair above
half drunk on the smell of turpentine.
Not a daub have I completed
since the heathers blackened. And yet I know
that but for the grace of my father's God
I could have painted like Gainsborough.

So — it is night, the tourists now all gone.
Relieved, the floorboards creak back into place.
None but we hear the long-dead clock;
for we are never, ever to be found
vaulted in the family tomb out there.
We are here, here
forever.

And it's gratifying to observe at the top of the stairs
someone took my quartered canvas from the attic,
unfolded it, and made me immortal.

Lewis Hosegood

Two Photographs of Top Withens

The house is ruinous enough, in my snapshot.
But most of the roofslabs are in place.
You sit holding your smile, in one of the sycamores.

We'd climbed from Stanbury.
And through all the leaves of the fierce book
To touch Wuthering Heights — a fouled nest.

My Uncle wrinkles his nose
At something distasteful.
Emily's dream has flown.

But you smile in the branches — still in your twenties,
Ear cocked for the great cries.
'We could buy this place and renovate it!'

Except, of course, except,
On second thoughts, maybe, except
For the empty horror of the moor —

Mad heather and grass tugged by the mad
And empty wind
That has petrified or got rid of

Everything but the stones.
The stones are safe, being stone.
Even the spirit of the place, like Emily's,

Hidden beneath stone.
Nothing's left for sightseers — only a book.
It was a blue day, with larks, when I aimed my
      camera.

We had all the time in the world.
Walt would live as long as you had lived.
Then the timeless eye blinked.
                              And weatherproofed,
Squared with Water Authority concrete, a roofless
Pissoir for sheep and tourists marks the site
Of my Uncle's disgust.
                        But the tree —
That's still there, unchanged beside its partner,
Where my camera held (for that moment) a ghost.

Ted Hughes

Whilst rejecting Charlotte's novel *The Professor*, however, Smith, Elder & Co wrote favourably to Charlotte about the work, discussing its merits and suggesting the author might write a book that would eventually be successful. They added that they would be prepared to give a work in three volumes careful attention. Charlotte immediately set about finishing *Jane Eyre*.

The highly perceptive reader at Smith, Elder was W S Williams, who read *Jane Eyre* and at once passed it on to George Smith, the publisher, who wrote:

> 'After breakfast on Sunday morning I took the MS of Jane Eyre
> to my little study and began to read it. The story quickly took me captive …
> I could not put the book down.'

The book was soon published and was an outstanding success, and Charlotte discovered Williams to be a valuable friend with whom she began to communicate regularly. Her sisters had found an unfortunate choice of publisher with T C Newby. The books were shabby and full of mistakes. However, both Emily and Anne remained loyal to their publisher, and all three novels were out by the winter of 1847. *Jane Eyre* was a great success. Thackeray had been sent a copy, and in a letter to Williams in October 1847 he says:

> 'I wish you had not sent me Jane Eyre. It interested me so much that I
> have lost (or won if you like) a whole day in reading it … '

Thackeray claimed he was familiar with the story of *Jane Eyre*, and Charlotte wrote to him saying she had thought it to be original. What she did not know was that Thackeray also had a wife who was mentally sick, as did Rochester in her novel.

Emily's novel *Wuthering Heights* provoked strong criticism. An unsigned review found in her desk after she had died says:

> ' … the reader is shocked, disgusted, almost sickened by details of cruelty,
> inhumanity and the most diabolical hate and vengeance, and even some
> passages of powerful testimony to the supreme power of love — even over
> demons in the human form … '

Strong words for Emily to take to the grave. Anne's *Agnes Grey* was received more gently: 'A simple tale of a governess's experience and trial of love, born with that meekness, and met by that fortitude, that ensures a final triumph … '

Heathcliff

Today she dreamed a man, delineated with her pen.
Before the ink was dry his eyelids lifted
and his black eyes shone.
She saw how she had stirred his heart.

His essence issues from the wind,
familiars: shadows, briars, the precipice.
His foot's a hoof.

His heartbeat comes within the body of a hawk.
Pen, paper, ink and thought have caught him,
tied him into words; a wretched animal,
enraged and cast within a trap.
And she, a wrist that rubs against a broken pane of glass,
and says the spirit's gist is also warm at last.

She dreams too fast,
and spirit touches flesh too much and cymbals clash,
and love is dashed, and roars the moor,
a hound possessed, a fiend,
its bloody gore a savageness she rides.

And the hawk's beak strives
to peck the eyes of pain.
It scales the cliff.
What need of flesh? Her spirit soars!

The owl screeches, and the night falls fast.
Curtainless, her window points the way to stars.
They too are rooted into rock, and gleam
an otherness, that seems like love.

Wendy Louise Bardsley

Class at Oakwell Hall, Birstall, Batley
(Fieldhead in Shirley)

They came to the museum for the day,
Hindus and Pakistanis and one African,
dark, vivid flames against English masonry,
bringing the light with them and flickering joy,
well-taught, good-mannered. So we tried, in play,
to share our heritage, to take a journey
difficult enough for the ordinary Englishman,
impossible, surely, for non-English girl and boy?

Through their hesitating postures Sam, the sheepdog, wove
an erratic tail-wagging path, and tentative hands
reached out against ancestral discipline
for dogs spread terror out in Pakistan,
scavenging in packs. And so we strove
without English words to reach their hearts, and win
that kind of confidence that understands
enduring affinities between man and man.

I, Mistress Meg, the housekeeper, took them, alone
through the rambling building, kindling a sense of age,
and reverence for it. I eased the panelling back
to reveal, hidden away, a different, older homestead,
timbered and plastered, inside the cladding stone;
showed them the spinning wheel and the men's boot-jack
and the secret cupboard like a safe for storage,
teasing, 'Don't tell the master everything I've said!'

They cooked a meal and made purple lavender bags,
pomanders, wax candles, tried quills on paper sheets
hand-pressed; then learned to spin from the raw wool.
They did dry-stone walling, and tumbled on the lawn
until, at the day's end, they dropped on the stone flags
(hot and exhausted) like a family at my feet,
while I told of ancient wars and a king forsworn.

Only as we left by the rarely used side door
where (under a porch) no more than a foot high
a tap drip-dripped into a sunken drain,
there a boy cried, 'But, that's just like Pakistan!'
and hall and garden vanished until I saw
a tiny village on a sun-scorched plain
with piped water, cool beneath a blistering sky,
fleetingly abandoned because of Ramadan.

What I had given, he gave to me again.

Mabel Ferrett

If This Be All

O God! if this indeed be all
  That Life can show to me;
If on my aching brow may fall
  No refreshing dew from Thee;

If with no brighter light than this
  The lamp of hope may glow
And I may only dream of bliss,
  And wake to weary woe;

If friendship's solace must decay,
  When other joys are gone,
And love must keep so far away,
  While I go wandering on, —

Wandering and toiling without gain,
  The slave of others' will,
With constant care and frequent pain,
  Despite, forgotten still;

Grieving to look on vice and sin,
  Yet powerless to quell
The current from within,
  The outward torrent's swell;

While all the good I would impart,
  The feelings I would share,
Are driven backward to my heart,
  And turned to wormwood there;

If clouds must ever keep from sight
  The glories of the Sun,
And I must suffer Winter's blight,
  Ere Summer is begun;

If Life must be so full of care —
  Then call me soon to Thee;
Or give me strength enough to bear
  My load of misery.

Anne Brontë

SECRET WORKS,
SICKNESS & SORROWS

The general opinion seems to have been that the Brontë sisters kept their novel-writing a secret in the parsonage. Patrick claimed he knew the girls were writing but did not interfere, and Mrs Gaskell tells a story of Charlotte, having taken *Jane Eyre* to her father, saying:

'Papa I've been writing a book.'

'Have you my dear?'

'Yes, and I want you to read it.'

'I am afraid it will try my eyes too much.

'But it is not in manuscript; it is printed.

'My dear! you've never thought of the expense it will be! It will be almost sure to be a loss, for how can you get a book sold? No one knows you or your name.'

'But papa, I don't think it will be a loss; no more will you, if you will just let me read you a review or two, and tell you more about it.'

It must have been a precious moment for Charlotte. After reading him several reviews she handed him the book, and some time later he commented to the others: 'Girls, do you know Charlotte has been writing a book, and it is much better than likely?'

The unscrupulous publishers of Anne and Emily's books, however, now saw a way in which they might boost their own sales by pretending their authors were the same person as the author of *Jane Eyre*, since at the time it was thought by many that this might be the case. By now the publishers of Charlotte's book wanted to know the truth, and Charlotte and Anne decided to make the journey to London to visit them, Emily, always less sociable, declining to go with them.

Emily Brontë

Was it always like this, or did
the crinoline have holes, the fingernails
bitten edges? Were there long periods
of nothing much at all, knocking
one stair's dust down to the next
and no words. Days when the graves went blind
by a sigh on a pane of glass, and the yew branch
scratted an empty afternoon mind.
When you decided you couldn't be bothered
to go bent head-first, onto the moors
but just stay at home and dream something
unimaginative, selfish, stereotyped.
Between bouts of red hot genius, to be
ordinary, relaxed, so that one could have
a conversation without shaking
with suppressed emotion.
Will heaven reveal this, or will it smooth
the gradient so much, it won't be you?

David Scott

Transvestism in the Novels of Charlotte Brontë

When reading Villette, Shirley and Jane Eyre
Though never somehow The Professor
Which was all too clear,
I used to overlook
The principal point of each book
As it now seems to me: what the characters wore.

Mr Rochester dressed up as the old crone
That perhaps he should have been,
De Hamal as a nun.
There was no need
For this. Each of them could
Have approached his woman without becoming one.

Not all heroines were as forthright.
Shirley in particular was a cheat.
With rakish hat
She strode like a man
But always down the lane
Where the handsome mill-owner lived celibate.

Lucy, however, knew just what she was doing.
And cast herself as a human being.
Strutting and wooing
In the school play
She put on a man's gilet,
Kept her own skirt, for fear of simplifying.

Their lonely begetter was both sister and brother.
In her dark wood trees do not scan each other
Yet foregather,
Branched or split,
Whichever they are not,
Whichever they are, and rise up together.

Patricia Beer

George Smith of the publishers Smith, Elder recollects the occasion of his meeting Currer and Acton Bell:

'I was at work in my room when a clerk reported that two ladies wished to see me. I was very busy and sent out to ask their names. The clerk returned to say that the ladies declined to give their names, but wished to see me on a private matter. Two rather quaintly dressed little ladies, pale-faced and anxious looking, walked into my room; one of them came forward and presented me with a letter addressed, in my own handwriting to "Currer-Bell Esq". I noticed that the letter had been opened and said with some sharpness, "Where did you get this from?" "From the Post Office", was the reply, "it was addressed to me. We have both come that you might have ocular proof that there are at least two of us". This then was "Currer Bell" in person. I need hardly say that I was at once keenly interested, not to say excited. Mr Williams was called down and introduced, and I began to plan all sorts of attention to our visitors.'

Of Charlotte's appearance, Smith says:

'I must confess that my first impression of Charlotte Brontë's personal appearance was that it was interesting rather than attractive. She was very small, and had a quaint old-fashioned look. Her head seemed too large for her body. She had fine eyes, but her face was marred by the shape of the mouth and by the complexion. There was but little feminine charm about her; and of this fact she herself was uneasily and perpetually conscious. It may seem strange that the possession of genius did not lift her above the weakness of an excessive anxiety about her personal appearance. But I believe she would have given all her genius and her fame to have been beautiful. Perhaps few women ever existed more anxious to be pretty than she, or more angrily conscious of the circumstances that she was not pretty'.

Anne, he said, was 'curiously expressive of a wish for protection and encouragement', and he described her as a quiet and gentle though

rather subdued person. The girls, however, found it difficult going to the opera at Covent Garden, as they were wearing old-fashioned high-necked dresses. It was a life that was completely unfamiliar to them and of which they felt no part.

Also they were constantly preoccupied as to what was going on at home and Branwell's miseries. He increasingly ran into debt, writing all the time to his friend Leyland about his troubles. Patrick and Charlotte attempted to help by paying off his debts, but his constant need for drugs and alcohol created an endless round of pain. Moreover, he was now in the relentless grip of tuberculosis.

Children of the Wind

We were children of the wind, growing for the sun.
But she must lock us in cellars of bone and ghost.

I have spent all my manhood on wrecking two families,
my poison is spent, overcome by some younger love.

I repent nothing. My heaven is a bed in the cold moor.
We will be frost and ice, will be again the lightning.

Glyn Wright

On the Death of Anne Brontë

There's little joy in life for me,
    And little terror in the grave;
I've lived the parting hour to see
    If one I would have died to save.

Calmly to watch the failing breath,
    Wishing each sigh might be the last;
Longing to see the shade of death
    O'er those beloved features cast.

The cloud, the stillness that must part
    The darling of my life from me;
And then to thank God from my heart,
    To thank Him well and fervently;

Although I knew that we had lost
    The hope and glory of our life;
And now, benighted, tempest-tossed,
    Must bear alone the weary strife.

On the 24th September 1848, Branwell died. The cause of death given as 'Marasmus — chronic bronchitis'. Charlotte was deeply disturbed and suffered greatly, writing to Williams of Smith, Elder & Co:

'When the struggle was over and a marble calm began to succeed the last agony, I felt, as I have never felt before, that there was peace and forgiveness for him in Heaven. All his errors — to speak plainly, all his vices — seemed nothing to me in that moment; every wrong he had done, every pain he had caused, vanished; his sufferings only were remembered; the wrench to the natural affections only was left.'

After Branwell's death, a dark cloud of illness seemed to spread through the parsonage. Anne became sick with asthma and Emily developed a persistent cough. Charlotte writes in October 1848:

'All the days of this winter have gone by darkly and heavily like a funeral train. Since September sickness has not quitted this house. It is strange it did not use to be so, but I suspect now all this has been coming on for years. Un-used, any of us, to the possession of robust health, we have not noticed the gradual approaches of decay; we did not know its symptoms; the little cough, the small appetite, the tendency to take cold at every variation of atmosphere, have been regarded as things of course. I see them in another light now.'

Emily deteriorated rapidly, refusing to call a doctor until the very end. She had never lingered over anything, Charlotte said, and now she made haste to leave. Emily died, at the age of thirty, on the 19th December 1848. She had struggled to the very end to dress herself, feed the dogs and carry out her usual tasks. On the day she died, Charlotte had searched the moors for a sprig of heather to give to her, but by the time she came back, Emily was lying on the sofa in the parlour dying. Charlotte wrote to Ellen Nussey on the 23rd December:

'Yes; there is not Emily in time or on earth now. Yesterday we put her poor, wasted mortal frame quietly under the chancel pavement ...'

And there was more to come, for Anne now coughed as Emily had done. Charlotte wrote to Smith, Elder & Co telling them that she could not write again until her sister had fully recovered her health and strength. Currer Bell was to be put on hold. George Smith sent regular boxes of books, reviews and journals to the parsonage, and re-issued the volume of poems the girls had produced.

Anne believed that better weather might heal her illness, and wanted to go to Scarborough where she might enjoy the sunshine and where she had previously worked as a governess. Ellen Nussey was to accompany her and Charlotte, and Charlotte felt it necessary at this time to forewarn her how emaciated Anne had become.

In York, Anne was able to see the Minster, and in Scarborough, where they lodged, she sat by the window looking at the sea. On Monday the 28th May 1849, aged twenty-nine, she died. Charlotte wrote that Anne had been happy to the last, and had died peacefully.

In less than a year, Charlotte had lost a brother and two sisters, and was completely devastated. She arranged for Anne to be buried at the old church in Scarborough to save Patrick the pain of another funeral.

Returning home in June to her lonely father and the two dogs, Keeper and Flossie, who had belonged to Emily and Anne, she wrote to Ellen:

> 'I call it home still … Keeper may visit Emily's little bedroom —
> as he still does day to day — and Flossie may still look wistfully
> round for Anne … '

Charlotte believed that labour was the only radical cure for rooted sorrow, but this time when she arrived home all the rooms were silent and empty. She felt desolate and bitter:

> 'The agony that was to be undergone and was not to be avoided
> came on. I underwent it, and passed a dreary evening and night,
> and a mournful morrow; today, I am better.'

Charlotte was now desperately lonely and unhappy. The 'exquisite bitterness' she speaks of in one of her letters — yet to be tasted — was now upon her. She writes to Ellen that 'the great trial is when evening closes and night approaches … '

Mr Brontë is Dying

'The man's bog-melancholy
needing an instrument
to draw it off —
and didn't he scull about
in the tipple

like a very leprechaun?
His was an Irishness
whiskey-flavoured. Dress
despoiler — boot-burner —
uncaring father.'

A droll epitaph, embellished now
with his own unspoken brogue.
Then he smiles. Picturing
that great congregation
of his friends asleep

on the hill-slope — as if a last
scouting of the climb's rigour
had drained their strength:
each grave a name, each name
a face with its special look.

Odd to have wallowed
in a reverie of salvation
induced by a bed's comfort,
and presumptuous to wonder
how many times, with the going —
down of this generous sun,
it might be reborn for his warming.

Ronald Tomkins

Last Lines

A dreadful darkness closes in
    On my bewildered mind:
O let me suffer and not sin,
    Be tortured yet resigned.

Through all this world of blinding mist
    Still let me look to thee,
And give me courage to resist
    The Tempter, till he flee.

Weary I am — O give me strength,
    And leave me not to faint;
Say thou wilt comfort me at length
    And pity my complaint.

I've begged to serve thee heart and soul,
    To sacrifice to Thee
No niggard portion, but the whole
    Of my identity.

I hoped amid the brave and strong,
    My portioned task might lie,
To toil amid the labouring throng
    With purpose keen and high;

But thou has fixed another part,
    And thou has fixed it well;
I said so with my breaking heart
    When first the anguish fell.

O thou has taken my delight
    And hope of life away,
And bid me watch the painful night
    And wait the weary day.

The hope and the delight were thine;
    I bless thee for their loan;
I gave thee while I deemed them mine
    Too little thanks I own.

Shall I with joy thy blessings share
    And not endure their loss;
Or hope the martyr's crown to wear
    And cast away the cross?

These weary hours will not be lost,
    These days of passive misery,
These nights of darkness, anguish-tost,
    If I can fix my heart on thee.

The wretch that weak and weary lies
    Crushed with sorrow, worn with pain,
Still to Heaven may lift his eyes
    And strive and labour not in vain;

Weak and weary though I lie
    Crushed with sorrow, worn with pain
I may lift to Heaven mine eye
    And strive and labour not in vain;

That inward strife against the sins
    That ever wait on suffering
To strike wherever first begins
    Each ill that would corruption bring;

That secret labour to sustain
    With humble patience every blow;
To gather fortitude from pain
    And hope and holiness from woe.

Thus let me serve thee from my heart
    Whate'er may be my written fate,
Whether thus early to depart
    Or yet a while to wait.

If thou shouldst bring me back to life,
    More humbled I should be,
More wise, more strengthened for the strife,
    More apt to lean on thee.

Should Death be standing at the gate,
    Thus should I keep my vow;
But hard whate'er my future fate,
    So let me serve thee now.

Anne Brontë

Scarborough: In Memory of Anne

Sooner or later it seems, each northern poet
pays tribute and tries their Brontë poem.
We thank Heaven for antibiotics,
yet feel the prick of jealousy, tragic death
being a tourist route to fame.
Even the father's grief is commercial,
worth a trip round some church
where once he blessed a child.
Anne we forget. Branwell with his booze
better suits our uneasy time.
Yet on this cliff, with sea and town beneath
it is Anne I think of, the gentle one.

She came here seeking health, and lies in death
apart, as in life. On this wall a plaque
names her grave. That is all.
A late thrush sings; waves whiten sand.
Few come, no one sells souvenirs.
Buried hurriedly and alone
Anne is the legend's footnote.
But she loved her moors too,
hated governessing, burnt with the same fire,
if less intensely. To die so far from home
would be cruel enough;
knowing she was second-rate a bitter death indeed.

Pauline Kirk

CHARLOTTE, NOVELS & MARRIAGE

Within the next three years Charlotte coped with her own and her father's illnesses, writing at the same time two more novels. She wrote to W S Williams of how the loss of the 'nearest and dearest' caused her to seek out what is left and, having found it, to hold on to it tenaciously:

> 'The faculty of imagination lifted me when I was sinking, three months ago. Its active exercise has kept my head above water since; its results cheer me now, for I feel they have enabled me to give pleasure to others. I am thankful to God, who gave me the faculty; and it is for me a part of my religion to defend this gift and to profit by its possession.'

Charlotte formed new friendships in London, making acquaintance with Sir James and Lady Kay Shuttleworth and Elizabeth Gaskell, and others who welcomed her to their houses and honoured her as a prized friend. Over the next few years she was to visit a variety of places in England and be entertained by distinguished people. Haworth Parsonage was soon known as the place where the famous author of *Jane Eyre* lived, and people would try to catch a glimpse of Charlotte. Around this time, however, she had felt uncomfortable at the parsonage. Its silent rooms reminded her of her lost brother and sisters, and the terrible sufferings she had witnessed. Even the moors began to make her feel melancholy. She and her father were often ill, and in 1851, Emily's dog Keeper died from natural causes. This was a blessing Charlotte said, since they had thought the dog might have to be 'put away' which none of them would have wanted to do.

Amongst Charlotte's admirers in Haworth was her father's curate, Arthur Bell Nicholls, who had taken on many of the parish responsibilities throughout her father's illness. In December, 1852, Mr Nicholls, who had come to love Charlotte very deeply, proposed. When she told her father he was outraged, calling the proposal 'that obnoxious subject'. This only served to arouse Charlotte's sympathy for Nicholls. She had declined three previous proposals but did not want her father to think she would remain unmarried forever.

Perhaps Patrick had good reason for wanting Charlotte to remain unmarried. He had lost his wife and five children. Charlotte was thirty-six and frail. A pregnancy might prove fatal; and in the end did. Also, the income she now obtained from her books brought her fifteen times that of Arthur Bell Nicholls and the laws of the day made a woman's property her husband's on marriage. Patrick was incensed. It would be to marry below her status, he thought, if she were to marry Arthur Bell Nicholls.

Charlotte's first consideration was one of love. She did not love Mr Nicholls. Patrick refused to see the man anyway and dealt with him by letter, treating him with scorn and contempt. Nicholls refused to be told to forget Charlotte and resigned his post.

Charlotte was able to identify with Nicholls' loneliness and felt sorry for him. He had made an application to go to Australia where he was going to become a missionary and had received excellent references from her father. The application was eventually withdrawn, however, and he stayed in Haworth.

Whilst delivering a service, on the 15th May 1853, with Charlotte in the congregation, she noted that he lost command of himself and began to shake. Fortunately Patrick Brontë was not there. Another day, on returning the deeds of the National school to Patrick, she found Nicholls weeping at the garden gate. Later Nicholls left them for the south of England, returning soon to Yorkshire again to be curate of Kirksmeaton near Pontefract.

Charlotte Nicholls

My husband smiles in sleep beside me;
The beck froths happily under Haworth hill,
And moonlight softens the wild tossing heather
On the frosty slopes towards Keighley.
Our coming child has stirred
In my womb, and perhaps I see now
What Emily never saw for the depth
Of her scarred isolation.
Warmth truth taps through the decay
Of the artist-urge: a curate's wife, living her vow,
Shames the impassioned fantasy.

If the years of deprivation
Were the years of deepest penetration,
If the sweet fulfilment
Bears me to the shallows, the content
Of common housewives in the village,
And the word that is everybody's word
Replaces the rare scribble on outcast rock —
I still choose the shared fulfilment, trusting
That the loss of the agonized gleam
is a mere loss of morbidity,
That the bright surface beyond purgation
Holds the abiding poetry.

I serve the Church, console the illiterate,
And learn what the black tempest could not teach,
Here or in Brussels. Emily's speech,
Aloof and cryptic, missed the ultimate
Which I seem to grasp in parish visitation.

In a city or on a moor,
The self-fulfilled alone are really poor.
The voice within the grim shell
Becomes imperious when its new mould is made,
But the friendly echo of a platitude
Uplifts the bereaved, the betrayed,
With fertilizing force denied to art.

I have watched, and fused with, in this parsonage,
Souls complex and original, who must bow
To the pang of finding that the rock-scrawl,
Rasped by the lightning or the ghostly finger,
Is always an extinct text
At faith's true dayspring — a nerve left to smart
In the eroded stoic heart.

I have been released indeed
From that aesthetic bondage
From the fume of fashioning, the loneliness
Of subtle planes where two worlds bleed
On the emerging mirror.
And I am thankful, for the fight was hard,
And Emily's end was terrible, I lie relaxed,
Warmed by my husband, and an owl hoots
Somewhere near the churchyard.
The wind may rise, straining the thorn-roots,
But a calm of ordinary bliss
Bears me to sleep unmarred.

Jack Clemo

Sketching From Life

As a woman, I am
Perfecting the art of the copyist —
Painting flowers from botanical plates —
Primula, convolvulus, digitalis purpurea.

As a man, I claim
Authorship of a novel,
Write to publishers
In businesslike phrases.

As a woman, I am skilled
In needlecraft. More exceptionally
In quilling: where tiny tolls of paper
Curl patience deep into pattern.

As a man I can collate
And promote my sisters' work —
Borrow masculinity for
Their burgeoning talents.

I sign A B, E B, C B —
the rhythm matches Emily's chant
From the kitchen, as she pummels the dough
And practises German verbs.

Today I am mourning my dead;
Wiping the dust from their names.
Beyond on the moors there is air,
And liberty, for sketching from life.

Frances Sackett

Patrick's new curate was by no means the match of Arthur Nicholls. He was neither reliable nor hard-working. Nicholls still wrote letters to Charlotte, which she hid from her father. She answered the letters and arranged to meet Nicholls secretly when next he came to stay with the Grants at Oxenhope, a village close to Haworth. In the meantime, she tried to persuade her father towards an appreciation of Arthur Nicholl's merits, and Patrick eventually allowed her to see him.

Charlotte now found herself in a relationship that was both giving and receiving. It might have been that the anguish she had suffered due to her unrequited love for M Heger had been advantageous to Nicholls, but he was soon reinstated as curate of Haworth and arrangements for marriage took place. They were to live in Haworth at the parsonage and continue to look after Patrick, who was becoming increasingly frail. Through marrying Nicholls and remaining in Haworth, she would hold on to something of her past and preserve what was left of her family life. They were married on Thursday the 29th June 1854, having a very quiet service with few guests. Patrick had refused to give Charlotte away, remaining in the house; Miss Wooler, Charlotte's former teacher and friend, taking the task over instead. Charlotte believed her father might have felt superstitious about the wedding and avoided it for that reason. The honeymoon was spent visiting his family home, Cuba House, at Banaghar in Ireland, where she found a family she liked beyond all her expectations. She writes to Ellen:

> *'My dear husband appears in a new light here in his own country. More than once I have had deep pleasure in hearing his praises on all sides. Some of the old servants and followers of the family tell me I am a most fortunate person for I have got one of the best gentlemen in the country … '*

At thirty-eight, Charlotte found herself happier than she had been for many years. A peat store was converted into a study for Arthur and she made curtains for the room.

Haworth Parsonage 1837

She lives close to death,
near the graveyard where her mother lies.
She reads poems on death, elegies cut in stone.

Words raise the dead,
disturb her father in his own room and world,
as he contemplates eternity.

But heaven is here.
She throws off the shawl that embalms her,
dashes outside to greet the Spring.

The wind embraces her,
lifts her skirt as she runs onwards.
Sunlight enters her and she conceives life.

Frost clings only to shadows now.
The stream thaws
and drives the millwheel of her heart.

Her words flow
across the manuscript of Haworth Moor,
cutting deep into memory.

Chris Woods

Haworth Churchyard

Where, behind Keighley, the road
Up to the heart of the moors
Between heath-clad showery hills
Runs, and colliers' carts
Poach the deep ways coming down,
And a rough, grimed race have their homes—

There on its slope is built
The moorland town. But the church
Stands on the crest of the hill,
Lonely and bleak; at its side
The parsonage-house and the graves.

Strew with laurel the grave
Of the early-daying! Alas,
Early she goes on the path
To the silent country, and leaves
Half her laurels unwon,
Dying too soon! — yet green
Laurels she had, and a course
Short, but redoubled by fame.

And not friendless, and not
Only with strangers to meet,
Faces ungreeting and cold,
Thou, O mourned one, to-day
Enterest the house of the grave!
Those of thy blood, whom thou lov'dst,
Have preceded thee — young,
Loving, a sisterly band;
Some in art, some in gift
Inferior — all in fame.
They, like friends, shall receive
This comer, greet her with joy;
Welcome thy sister, thy friend;
Hear with delight of thy fame!

Round thee thy lie — the grass
Blows from their graves toward thine!
She, whose genius, though not
Puissant like thine, was yet
Sweet and graceful; and she
(How shall I sing her?) whose soul
Knew no fellow for might,
Passion, vehemence, grief,
Daring, since Byron died,
That world-famed son of fire — she, who sank
Baffled, unknown, self-consumed;
Whose too bold dying song
Stirred, like a clarion-blast, my soul.

Of one, too, I have heard,
A brother — sleeps he here?
Of all that gifted race
Not the least gifted; young,
Unhappy, eloquent — the child
Of many hopes, of many tears.
O boy, if here thou sleep'st sleep well!
On thee too did the Muse
Bright in thy cradle smile;
But some dark shadow came
(I know not what) and interposed.

Sleep, O cluster of friends,
Sleep! — or only when May,
Brought by the west-wind, returns
Back to your native heaths,
And the plover is heard on the moors,
Yearly awake to behold
The opening summer, the sky,
The shining moorland — to hear
The drowsy bee, as of old,
Hum o'er the thyme, the grouse
Call from the heather in bloom!
Sleep, or only for this
Break your united repose!

Matthew Arnold

The Brontë Museum

Lines from the *Keighley Herald* on the opening of the
Museum, May 24th 1895. Most respectfully dedicated
to Sir Thomas Wemyss Reid.

Oh! bring me again the harp of old Ebor,
For rusty and dusty it long hath been hung;
Let me tune it once more I ask as a favour —
That harp which no minstrel lately hath strung.

It is not a pean by the aid of Apollo,
For lo! my plain muse cannot soar up so high;
Yet though persevere, and others will follow,
For the praise of the Brontës should reach to the sky.

Charlotte Brontë great Jove's gifted daughter;
The genius of Worth and star of her sex;
Nature's own nymph, as pure as the water;
The world is beginning to pay thee respects.

And this, the event — a humble beginning —
In honour of thee — the museum today;
And proud they will be, to read the first inning,
Over the ocean in lands far away.

Bill o' th' Hoylus End

However, Charlotte's happiness was again to be curtailed. She became pregnant, and whilst out walking on the moors was chilled in a rainstorm. By the following February she was seriously ill. During this time Tabitha died, the old nurse who had been with the Brontë family for over thirty years. Charlotte suffered both mentally and physically:

'I strain until what I vomit is mixed with blood … As to my husband — my heart is knit to him — he is tender, so good, helpful, patient … '

Patrick wrote to Ellen Nussey, telling her there was no hope for Charlotte:

'We have only to look forward to the solemn event, with prayer to God and he will give us grace and strength sufficient unto the day…'

Patrick asked Ellen if she would be kind enough to write to Charlotte's friends Miss Wooler and Mrs Taylor and let them know. Charlotte died on Saturday the 31st March 1855, in the early hours. She had said, on hearing her husband praying by her side:

'Oh, I am not going to die, am I? He will not separate us, we have been so happy.'

The cause of death was recorded as Phthisis, a consumptive and wasting disease of the tissues.

The parsonage was to be the home of Arthur Bell Nicholls and Patrick Brontë until the old man died on the 7th June 1861, aged eighty-five. By this time the Brontë story had already become legend. Mrs Gaskell, Charlotte's friend, wrote an account of Charlotte's life, Patrick carefully reading what was to be printed, and this has been a source of great interest and pleasure to Brontë enthusiasts all over the world. When Patrick died, Arthur Bell Nicholls sold the parsonage's household contents and returned to Ireland. The Brontë family had been in Haworth for over forty years. By 1862 they had all gone.

Charlotte Brontë's Grave

All overgrown by cunning moss,
All interspersed with weed,
The little cage of 'Currer Bell'
In quiet 'Haworth' laid.

This bird — observing others
When frosts too sharp became
Retire to other latitudes —
Quietly did the same — .

But differed in returning —
Since Yorkshire hills are green —
Yet not in all the nests I meet —
Can Nightingale be seen —

Or —

Gathered from many wanderings —
Gethsemane can tell
Thro' what transporting anguish
She reached the Asphodel!

Soft fall the sounds of Eden
Upon her puzzled ear —
Oh what an afternoon for Heaven,
When 'Brontë' entered there!

Emily Dickinson

LIST OF POEMS & PHOTOGRAPHS

NOTE: Poems references are printed in a serif typeface; and pictures in a sans serif typeface.

24
'Haworth Parsonage, Mt Maunganui' by Janet Frame. From *The Pocket Mirror*, The Women's Press, 1967. Reproduced by permission of Curtis Brown Ltd, London, on behalf of Janet Frame 1967.
Haworth from the south-east, from Whiteley Turner's *A Spring Time Saunter*, 1913.

25
'Visit to Haworth' by Shelagh Florey. From *Poetry Introduction 8*, Faber & Faber, 1993.
Erecting Japanese language footpath signs on Haworth Moor, 1991 (Simon Warner).

26
'Haworth' by Ridley Beeton. Brontë Society Publications, Keighley, 1970.
Geese in flight, upper Worth Valley (Simon Warner).

27
Haworth Parsonage and church as the Brontës would have known them, as shown by the lack of trees in the churchyard (Brontë Society).

28
'Haworth Moor' by James Waddington. From *The Poets of Keighley, Bingley, Haworth and District*, ed C F Forshaw, 1893.
Heather on Haworth Moor (Simon Warner).

29
'Brontë Bridge' by Pauline Kirk. First published in *Aireings* and *Poetry Monash* (Australia), 1989.
Brontë Bridge (Simon Warner).

30
Cotton grass on Brow Moor (Simon Warner).

31
'Brontë Way' by Jean Barker. From *Footsteps on a Journey*, Aireings Publications, 1994.

32
Aunt Branwell (Brontë Society).

33
'High Waving Heather' by Emily Brontë. From *The Brontës: Selected Poems*, ed Juliet Barker, Everyman Classics, 1985.
Heather, Haworth Moor (Simon Warner).

34
Ring ouzel by Emily Brontë, 22nd May 1829 (Brontë Society).

35
'Gondal' by Lewis Hosegood. From *Wreathes of Snow, a Brontë Poem Cycle*, Orlando Press, 1994.
Little book by Charlotte Brontë, 1830 (Brontë Society).

36
'Retrospection' by Charlotte Brontë. From *The Brontë Sisters Selected Poems*, ed Stevie Davies, Carcanet, 1976.

37
Beside Sladen Beck, Haworth Moor (Simon Warner).

38
'Cowan Bridge Boarding School' by Peggy Poole. 1997. Reproduced by permission of the author.
Cowan Bridge School (Simon Warner).

39
'At Cowan Bridge' by U A Fanthorpe. From *A Watching Brief*, Peterloo Poets, 1987.

40
'Thorp Green' by Branwell Brontë. From *Unpublished Poems*, Caxton Press, 1927.
Sun through the mist at Ponden Reservoir (Simon Warner).

41
'Alone I Sat' by Emily Brontë. From *The Brontës: Selected Poems*, ibid.

42
On Penistone Hill (Simon Warner).

43
'The Phenomenon' by Patrick Brontë, an extract. From 'Earthquake on the Moors', a pamphlet, 1824.

44-45
'Branwell Brontë is Re-incarnated as a Vest' by Ian McMillan. 1995. Reproduced permission of the author.
Moon over Whitestone Clough (Simon Warner).

46
Sycamores at Top Withens (Simon Warner).

47
'Charlotte Brontë' by Susan Coolidge (Sarah Chauncey Woolsey). From *The Oxford Book of Children's Verse in America*, ed Donald Hall, Oxford University Press, 1985.

76-77
'I'll Come When Thou Art Saddest' by Emily Brontë. From *The Brontës: Selected Poems*, ibid.
Haworth Parsonage and church in snow (Simon Warner).

78
'A Place for Beginnings' by Mabel Ferrett. From *The Taylors of the Red House*, Kirklees Leisure Services, 1987.

79
The Red House, Gomersal (Simon Warner).

80-81
'The Teacher's Monologue' by Charlotte Brontë. From *The Brontës: Selected Poems*, ibid.
Hill End Farm (now demolished), Haworth Moor (Simon Warner).

82
Spring in the Worth Valley (Simon Warner).

83
'Ellen Nussey Observes' by Lewis Hosegood. Ibid.

84
'Parting' by Charlotte Brontë. From *The Brontës: Selected Poems*, ibid.

85
Scar Hill, Haworth Moor (Simon Warner).

86
Winter morning with setting sun, Haworth Moor and Worth Valley (Simon Warner).

87
'Looking for Heathcliff' by Frances Nagle. From *Steeplechase Park*, Rockingham Press, 1996.

88
Pennine winter moorland (Simon Warner).

89
'Emily Brontë' by Cecil Day-Lewis. From *The Golden Treasury of Best Songs and Lyrical Poems in the English Language*, ed F T Palgrave, OUP, 1964.

91
'I Love the Silent Hour' by Anne Brontë. *From Exiled and Harassed Anne*, Raymond Ernest, Brontë Society Publications, Caxton Press, 1949.
Gate, moorland edge above Oxenhope (Simon Warner).

92-93
'Yes Thou Art Gone' by Anne Brontë. From *The Brontës: Selected Poems*, ibid.
'Severed and Gone' by Anne Brontë. From *The Brontës: Selected Poems*, ibid.
Far Westfield, Haworth Moor (Simon Warner).

94
'A Valentine' by the Brontë sisters. From *The Brontës: Selected Poems*, ibid.

95
Stanbury from Hob Hill (Simon Warner).

96
Scar Hill, Haworth Moor (Simon Warner).

97
'Emily' by Jean Barker. From *Footsteps on a Journey*, Aireings Publications, 1994.

98
Portrait of Charlotte Brontë by J H Thompson (Brontë Society).

99
Comic sketch by Charlotte Brontë, 6th March 1843 (Brontë Society).

100
'In the Brontë Museum, Haworth' by Sally Carr. First published in *Spokes*, summer 1994.

101
Parsonage dining room (Brontë Society).

102-103
'Three' by Anne Carson, an extract from *The Glass Essay*. First published in *Raritan*, New Jersey, USA. Reproduced by permission of the author.
Dogs and Bread' by Annie Foster. From *Flambard New Poets*.
Soup tureens at Ponden Hall, Stanbury (Simon Warner).

104
'Patrick Brontë' by Mary Hodgson. Reproduced by permission of the author.

105
Stanbury Church (Simon Warner).

106
From 'Reason' by Charlotte Brontë. From *The Brontë Sisters Selected Poems*, ed Stevie Davies, Carcanet, 1976.
Haworth Church (Simon Warner).

107
'He Saw My Heart's Woe' by Charlotte Brontë. From *The Brontës: Selected Poems*, ibid.

108
Self-portrait by Branwell Brontë, c1840 (Brontë Society).

110
'Emily' by Alison Chisholm. 1995. By permission of the author.
Emily Brontë's writing desk (Brontë Parsonage).

111
'Jane' by Kathleen Jamie. From *The Way We Live*, Bloodaxe Books, 1987.

112
Monk's House, Thorp Green, Little Ouseburn, North Yorkshire (Simon Warner).

113
'Lines Written at Thorp Green' by Anne Brontë. From *The Brontës: Selected Poems*, ibid.

114
'The Brontë Brother' by Gerard Woodward. From *Householder*, Chatto & Windus, 1991.

115
'Mourning Ring' by Ian Emberson. Envoi Publications 102, 1992.
Haworth Moor (Simon Warner).

116-117
'The Consolation' by Anne Brontë. From *The Brontës: Selected Poems*, ibid.
'Home' by Anne Brontë. From *The Brontës: Selected Poems*, ibid.
Snow, upper Worth Valley (Simon Warner).

118-119
'Wuthering Heights' by Sylvia Plath. From *Crossing the Water*, Harper Collins, 1962.
Haworth Moor: the way to Top Withens (Simon Warner).

120
'Branwell' by William Oxley. 1995. Reproduced by permission of the author.

121
'Branwell Speaks' by Lewis Hosegood. Ibid.
Snow, upper Worth Valley (Simon Warner).

122
'Two Photographs of Top Withens' by Ted Hughes. From *Elmet*, Faber & Faber, 1994.
Top Withens (Simon Warner).

124
'Heathcliff' by Wendy Louise Bardsley. From *Amphitheatre*, Rockingham Press, 1996.

125
After-glow with trees, Worth Valley (Simon Warner).

126
'Class at Oakwell Hall, Birstall, Batley' by Mabel Ferrett. From *Scattered Earth*, University of Salzburg, 1996.

127
Colne Valley Museum, Golcar, near Huddersfield (Simon Warner).

128-129
'If This Be All' by Anne Brontë. From *The Brontës: Selected Poems*, ibid.
Frost over the Sladen Valley (Simon Warner).

131
'Emily Brontë' by David Scott. 1994. Reproduced by permission of the author.
Patrick Brontë's study (Brontë Society).

132
'Transvestism in the Novels of Charlotte Brontë' by Patricia Beer. From *Collected Poems*, Carcanet, 1990.

133
Alcomden Stones (Simon Warner).

134
The 'Bell' signatures (Brontë Society).

135
'Children of the Wind' by Glyn Wright. 1996. Reproduced by permission of the author.
Brontë Parsonage and Sunday school (Simon Warner).

136
Portrait of Anne Brontë by Charlotte Brontë, 17th April 1833 (Brontë Society).

'On the Death of Anne Brontë' by Charlotte Brontë. From *The Brontës: Selected Poems*, ibid.

137
'Mr Brontë is Dying' by Ronald Tomkin. From *Lancaster Literature Festival Poems*, 1994.

138
'Last Lines' by Anne Brontë. From *The Brontës: Selected Poems*, ibid.

139
'Scarborough: In Memory of Anne' by Pauline Kirk. Aireings Publications and Poetry Monash (Australia), 1989.
Anne Brontë's grave, Scarborough (Simon Warner).

141
Arthur Bell Nichols, c1861 (Brontë Society).

142
'Charlotte Nicholls' by Jack Clemo. From *The Naked Astronaut: Poems on Birth and Birthdays*, ed R Graziani, Faber & Faber, 1983.

143
Heather in bloom, Haworth Moor (Simon Warner).

144
'Sketching from Life' by Frances Sackett. 1996. Reproduced by permission of the author.

145
'Haworth Parsonage 1837' by Chris Woods. From *Recovery*, Enitharmon Press, 1993.
Churchyard path to the moors, Haworth (Simon Warner).

146
Haworth from Brow Moor (Simon Warner).

147
'Haworth Churchyard' by Matthew Arnold. From *The Faber Book of Poems and Places*, ed Geoffrey Grigson, Faber & Faber, 1980.

148
'The Brontë Museum' by Bill o' th' Hoylus End. First published in the *Keighley Herald*, 24th May 1895.
Main Street, Haworth (Brontë Society).

149
'Charlotte Brontë's Grave' by Emily Dickinson. From *The Poems of Emily Dickinson* vol 1, ed Thomas H Johnson, Harvard University Press, 1955.

INDEX OF POEMS & AUTHORS

TED HUGHES OBE

1930 — 1998

Poet Laureate